I Hate Giving Presentations!

Your essential confidence booster

Michael D. Owen

Published by Fenman, Clive House, The Business Park, Ely, Cambs, CB7 4EH

Tel: 013563 665533 Fax: 01353 663644 E-mail: fenman@dial.pipex.com
Website: http: www.fenman.co.uk

First published 1997

British Library in Publication Data

A record for this book is available from the British Library

ISBN 1 872 483 38 0

Printed by Advanced Laser Press, St Ives

Cover design by Jane Norman, Cambridge

Fenman is a trademark of Fenman Ltd

Your personal record

As you work through this book, you will be asked to record your thoughts and experiences on successful presentation. You can make it your personal reference book by adding to these thoughts as you get more experience and see others using techniques which you think work well.

The relevant frames are noted below, with page numbers, so that you can find them easily.

You may also wish to record your name, address etc:

Name _____

Address _____

_____

_____

Telephone _____

E-Mail _____

What is a presentation?	6
What makes a presentation poor?	9
What makes a presentation good?	11
Tips on how to control nerves	19
Your communication movements	28
Knowing *Super You*	31
Keeping the audience listening	35
Body language signals	37
How you prepared to persuade	43
Purposes of presentations	45
Tailoring for the audience	50
Factors affecting the end result	56
Techniques for grabbing attention	77
Effective use of visual aids	88
Ineffective handling of questions	97
Successful handling of questions	106

About the author

Michael D. Owen has extensive first-hand experience of giving all types of presentations, both as a trainer and as a speaker at International Conventions. His training and coaching programmes have helped thousands of people to improve their presentation skills over the last 30 years.

Following a successful career in BTR, Kodak, Abbey National and in the travel and tourism industry he set up his own training consultancy in 1982. Its client list covers a wide range of organisations from small to multinational in Britain, Europe and the Middle East. Assignments successfully carried out have encompassed a diverse range of industries including construction, electronics, finance, medical, public relations, telecommunications, television and tourism.

He is a Fellow of The Institute of Personnel & Development, a Member of The Chartered Institute of Marketing and has been awarded Honorary Membership of The City & Guilds of London Institute.

Table of contents

	They want you to give a presentation!	1
1	**Introduction**	
1.0	Putting a presentation into perspective	5
1.1	What is a presentation?	6
1.2	What you have learned from others	9
1.3	Achieving the good points	13
2	**Powerful Presenting**	
2.0	Introduction	15
2.1	Making nerves work *for* you	16
	Keynotes: Making nerves work *for* you	23
2.2	Projecting confidence	24
2.3	The PLUS factor	29
2.4	Keeping them listening	33
	Keynotes: Powerful presenting	41
3	**The Strategy for Success**	
3.0	Introduction	43
3.1	Identify the purpose	45
3.2	Specify the audience	49
3.3	Test for success	54
3.4	The PLY approach	59
	Keynotes: The strategy for success	62
4	**The Structure for Success**	
4.0	Introduction	63
4.1	Conclusion	69
4.2	Developing the body	70
4.3	Attractive introduction	77
	Keynotes: The structure for success	82
5	**From Content to Presentation**	
5.0	Introduction	83
5.1	Visual aids	86
	Keynotes: Visual aids	96
5.2	Handling questions	97
	Keynotes: Handling questions	107
5.3	Take control	108
5.4	And finally . . .	109
Appendices		
A	In advance checklist	111
B	On the day checklist	112
C	For further reading	113

They want you to give a presentation!

You are asked to give a presentation. Do you accept and look forward to the challenge? Or do you:

- Accept with a feeling of dread?
- Think who else you could get to do it?
- Suddenly find that you have another pressing engagement?

Or have people stopped asking you because they know you will refuse?

No doubt you often hear people say *I hate giving presentations!* – perhaps you have said it yourself. Why is this? In reality, most people are apprehensive of giving a presentation: a survey asking what people were most scared of revealed public speaking at the top of the list.

This means that some people:

- Avoid doing it but miss out on opportunities which presenting could give them.
- Try to avoid it but find that they do not always escape and cannot give their best because of inexperience.
- Are prepared to give it a go but feel that they could do it rather better.

If any of these apply to you, the material in this book is designed to help. Indeed you may even find that you *can enjoy* giving presentations, if you give yourself the chance!

How you can use this book

As a self-study programme

In Section 2 you learn how to develop the techniques of delivery. In Sections 3, 4 and 5, you will develop a presentation using a step by step sequence.

As you work through the material you will find two types of exercise:

 The pencil sign indicates an exercise asking you to think about your experience of presentation; everyone has this, if only as a member of an audience. Frames are provided for you to record the answers.

Several of the exercises ask you to record things that you have seen which have helped to make a presentation successful. Your record need not stop with what you have seen so far; you can add to the frames as you see more good examples in the future. Learning about presentation should never stop; you can always benefit from your own experience and from watching others.

The arrow sign indicates an exercise for you to practise and, preferably, get feedback on from friends and/or colleagues. You will find it useful to repeat some of these exercises from time to time as a refresher (see below).

For each exercise: Once you have written down your answers in the frames, turn to the next page for our suggestions. If you feel tempted to look at the suggestions first, cover them up!

As a handbook

If you have to give a presentation you can either work through the text as you prepare it, starting at Section 3.0, or use the Keynotes at the end of each part, referring to the text when necessary. The Keynotes summarise the main points in the text. Each Keynote has a cross reference showing where to find supporting information in the text.

As a refresher

We never achieve perfection in using a skill: even the top sports professionals have, from time to time, to modify the grip they use or how they play a particular stroke. It's the same for the presenter. You can use the Keynotes and the practical exercises to help you to review your strengths and develop your presentation skills further.

The help you can get

Friends/Colleagues

Some of the material, particularly in Section 2, is about how you came across to others. Your friends and colleagues can help you with feedback on this. There are also exercises which ask you to get information from them. Discussing presentations and the content of this workbook will help you to develop your understanding of what is involved.

For some of you, this may be enough. Others may appreciate more assistance. We, therefore, offer the following back-up services to help you to develop your presentation skills and/or tackle your presentations.

Video Feedback

Send a videotape of one of your presentations to the author. You will receive a report highlighting the strong points, prioritised points for you to develop and recommendations on how to achieve this.

The charge for this is £20 for a presentation of less than 15 minutes; £25 for a presentation of between 15 and 25 minutes or £1 per minute for a presentation of more than 25 minutes.

Send your videotape and cheque to Michael D Owen, *Training Plus*, Edenbank House, 54 Pheasants Way, Rickmansworth, Hertfordshire WD3 2HA. Please include the following information:

About you: your name, address and telephone/fax number;

About the presentation: its purpose, the audience (see Section 3.2), background (eg overall length, formal/informal).

Follow-up workshop

Presentation courses which allow the opportunity for each participant to practise usually take *two or three days*. If you have been through this workbook and are interested in attending a one-day Fenman course on this topic, please telephone Fenman Limited on 01353 665533 to register your interest. Courses will be run according to demand.

1
Introduction

1.0 *Putting a presentation into perspective*

1.1 *What is a presentation?*

1.2 *What you have learned from others*

1.3 *Achieving the good points*

1.0 Putting a presentation into perspective

They want you to give a presentation, but just what do they have in mind?

For some, a presentation can be having to say a few words to introduce an item at a meeting. For others, it may be standing on a platform for an hour or more addressing hundreds of people. In Section 1.1, we:

- Start with a definition of a presentation, and

- Go on to note the similarities and differences between it and normal conversation.

You already have presentation experience, even if only as a member of an audience. In Section 1.2, you:

- Have the opportunity to review what you have learned from this experience, and to focus on the good points you have noted about successful presentations.

In Section 1.3, we outline the structure we will work with to achieve these good points in this workbook.

1.1 What is a presentation?

 We'll try one of those exercises now. 'Presentation' is one word which is used to cover many activities which seem to be very different. Just think of all the different situations which might involve someone presenting to one or more people and list them in the frame below.

Types of presentations

Here are some examples of presentations:

> A speech to a large audience using the latest technology in audiovisuals
> Telling a new employee how to do the job
> Team briefing
> Speech at a party political conference
> Putting an idea forward to the boss
> Showing a party of visitors around
> Instructing a group on a new system
> A wedding speech
> Reporting back on a meeting
> Showing a friend how to do something
> Trying to sell to a customer
> Making a recommendation to the Board
> Training a group
> An after dinner speech.

You have probably got others on your list.

Many people might not regard some of the items on the list as presentations. One of the main reasons for this is that they tend to think of presentations as formal events, like public speaking. They don't have to be: in The Oxford English Dictionary a presentation is defined as:

The action of presenting something to the mind or mental perception, a description, a statement.

(Source: *The New Shorter Oxford English Dictionary,* Fourth Edition, 1993, reproduced by permission of Oxford University Press.)

The definition includes all the items on the list except, perhaps, the after dinner speech and wedding speech. These certainly call for skills in presenting to others.

We will use as our working definition of presentation:

Any activity which involves speaking with a purpose to an audience of one or more.

The key factor is: *with a purpose.* The purpose may vary considerably, and so will the type of presentation. For example, making a recommendation to the Board is very different to making an after dinner speech, but both have a purpose. The purpose of making the recommendation is to get it accepted; that of the after dinner speech is to entertain and possibly to propose a toast.

Achieving the purpose involves having to speak for longer than is necessary in an ordinary conversation, whether the occasion is formal or informal. Look at what happens in a normal conversation:

You say something, but you don't speak for long – usually a matter of seconds. The other person speaks or interjects, again not for long.

In a normal conversation one person does not usually listen to another for more than a minute. So what happens if someone speaks to you for two or three minutes? Usually you stop listening although you would be prepared to listen to some people for longer than others. Similarly, they would stop listening to you although how quickly depends on your own skill in presenting.

If you are giving a presentation to achieve a purpose you cannot afford to let the audience stop listening. That's where your presentation skills have to be used more than usual.

Note that we *are* talking about skills that you already have. There are probably several items on the list which you do quite comfortably, like showing a friend how to do something or putting forward an idea.

Achieving the purpose of your presentation requires you to use your skills more powerfully and, possibly, to develop some new ones. It's rather like running: you can run although this may be not very far and not very fast; if you wanted to achieve a better result you would need to develop your skill.

So, the purpose of this workbook is to help you to:

- Realise the skills you already have and develop them further.

- Use them flexibly and appropriately in different types of presentation.

- Develop new techniques which would enhance your presentation.

1.2 What you have learned from others

Think about the presentations you have heard or seen which you thought were poor.

- What did the presenter do or not do?
- How did they come across?
- What about the content?

Note in the frame below why you thought the presentation was poor. There are no right or wrong answers – they are a matter of personal opinion.

Presentations were poor because

The most common reasons given for calling a presentation poor are:

The bad points	Symptoms
☒ Nerves	Mannerisms: e.g. repetitive movement such as swaying from side to side, playing with pen etc; Persistent clearing of throat.
☒ Inadequate preparation	Didn't know 'their lines'; Lost their way.
☒ Difficult to follow	Jumped from one point to another; Backtracked over the same points; Too much to take in at a time.
☒ Pitched at the wrong level	From '*couldn't understand*' to '*teaching grandmother to suck eggs*'.
☒ Alienating the audience	Inappropriate humour; Politically incorrect; Patronising.
☒ Boring	Monotonous delivery; Content dull; Waffling.
☒ Too long	No further comment needed!
☒ Visual aids wrong	Didn't know how to operate visual aid equipment; Got in the way of the screen; Visual aids didn't work; Visual aids were shown in the wrong order or the wrong way round; Print was too small to read.
☒ Lost control	Member(s) of the audience (e.g. questioner) took over; Failed to deal with interruptions.
☒ Thrown by questions	Didn't know answers; Didn't answer questions properly.

Now think about the presentations you have seen or heard which you thought were good and note in the frame below why you thought so.

Again there are no right or wrong answers – just note down what you think.

Presentations were good because

Some of your answers may be the opposite of those which made a presentation poor. You may also have introduced several new factors. The points most often mentioned are:

The good points	**Symptoms**
☑ *Very confident*	Looked at ease; No distracting signs of nerves.
☑ *Fluent*	Never at a loss for words; No awkward pauses.
☑ *Enthusiastic about the subject*	Lively speaker; Animated.
☑ *Time flew by*	Never bored.
☑ *Kept the audience involved*	Got them doing things rather than just sitting.
☑ *In tune with the audience*	Geared to the audience's viewpoint; Aware of audience reactions.
☑ *Pitched at the right level*	Neither lost the audience nor talked down to them.
☑ *Easy to understand*	One point followed another logically; Explained clearly; Organised into easily digestible sections.
☑ *Made it interesting/come to life*	Included personal interest points; Never just a catalogue of facts.
☑ *Entertaining/humorous*	Used humour appropriately.
☑ *Appropriate visual aids*	Imaginative; Constructively used to help get the message across.
☑ *Kept in control*	Never let the audience take over; Answered the questions well.

These good points apply to all types of presentation; our aim is to achieve them across the board.

1.3 Achieving the good points

The text in this workbook has been structured around the good points noted on the previous page:

Good point

Achieving it

Very confident
Fluent
Enthusiastic about the subject

These points are about how you come across to your audience and how you interact with them. We look at this in:

Time flew by
Kept the audience involved
In tune with the audience

Section 2: Powerful Presenting, putting it across with confidence and conviction.

Pitched at the right level
Easy to understand
Made it interesting/come to life
Entertaining/humorous

Powerful Presenting is important for success but it cannot cover up shortfalls in the content. These will adversely affect the audience and undermine the confidence of the presenter. Thus, **Powerful Presenting** is complemented by:

Section 3: The Strategy for Success, how to set about planning a successful presentation, and

Section 4: The Structure for Success, deciding what to include and exclude and putting it into a structure.

Appropriate visual aids
Kept in control

Planning gets the strategy and content right, but that is not enough for powerful presenting and keeping control. Achieving these involves further preparation which we consider in:

Section 5: From Content to Presentation, the steps involved in preparing for your presentation once you've decided on its content.

2
Powerful Presenting

2.0 Introduction

2.1 Making nerves work for *you*

2.2 Projecting confidence

2.3 The PLUS factor

2.4 Keeping them listening

2.0 Introduction

In this Section of the workbook we look at the impact you have on your audience and how to increase it. The information is relevant to all presentation, whether the audience is just one person, say an interviewer, or hundreds. Remember, we have identified that when presenting you have to hold attention for longer than is necessary in an ordinary conversation. So you need extra power for all presenting, although how much depends on the situation; if the audience is small you do not want to overpower them.

You cannot achieve Powerful Presenting if you are overcome with nerves so we look at this problem first in Section 2.1 Making nerves work *for* you.

Powerful Presenting requires:

Projecting confidence   How to achieve this is described in Section 2.2.

The PLUS factor   This is explained in Section 2.3.

Keeping them listening   Something you have to do to be successful. It partly depends on the confidence you project and the PLUS factor but even these have their limits. In Section 2.4 we consider other techniques that you can use.

2.1 Making nerves work *for* you

While most people feel quite comfortable when showing a friend how to do something, they are afraid of public speaking. We have already noted (page 1) the survey which showed that public speaking creates more fear than anything else. The more challenging presentations which you have to give will involve overcoming the nerve factor, so let's look at how to tackle it.

2.1.1 Nerves are good for presentations!

If only you could get the experience, you could be like those professionals who obviously aren't nervous. It's what many people think but actually it's **not** true.

But what about the *real* professionals? Those actors, musicians etc. who show that with experience the nerves go away. In fact, most people who perform frequently in public say that they still get nerves before they 'go on'. Opera singer Jessye Norman once described it as a wonderful thing to feel nervous when you are going to perform for an audience. Some famous professional performers are even physically sick before every performance!

> The professional knows:
>
> • That feeling nervous is **necessary** if you are to give your best
> • Their nerves have a **positive** effect.

Feeling nervous increases the flow of adrenaline. This helps you to:

• Present with greater energy, and

• Speed up your thinking; invaluable when you have to think on your feet!

Note that we have used the word *nerves* not *fear*. Some will point out that fear is caused by nerves, but there is a difference of degree. Fear is extreme nervousness, which gets in the way of a good performance. Nerves, on the other hand, help to sharpen performance.

So accept that you will and should feel nervous: it's part of the package for doing your best.

But how can you possibly do your best when your stomach is churning, your heart is pounding and your trembling legs feel like jelly? This is where we come to the professionals' secret.

> The professionals' secret is:
>
> • They don't *appear* to be nervous.

That's all very well but it does not answer the question of how they achieve it. How can *you* do it?

2.1.2 WYFI*N*WOS

What **Y**ou **F**eel **I**s *Not* **W**hat **O**thers **S**ee

- You are nervous.
- You *think* the audience can see how terrible you feel.
- In fact you could not possibly look as bad as you feel!

Realising this is *true* is the key to appearing confident even when you feel nervous.

I remember getting a pre-course questionnaire from a delegate who was going to come on one of my courses in which he said: "I hate presentations, just completing this questionnaire gives me a feeling of dread about attending the course."

Yet he was experienced at giving presentations and had been overseas several times to give presentations which had been successful in persuading people to spend millions of pounds.

After the first presentation he gave, the reaction of his colleagues was: "What are you doing here? You don't need any training."

> # WYFI*N*WOS
>
> • You can look very different to how you feel.
>
> • You usually look much better than you feel.

Most people find this very difficult to believe. I have heard the following conversation between a presentation course delegate and their fellow participants on numerous occasions:

> "It's all right for you but I get really nervous."

> "What makes you think you're so different, we're nervous too."

> "No you aren't, I can see you aren't."

> "But we can see that you aren't."

Fortunately, video can now prove to the doubters that they really are coming across far better than they think.

In addition, there are things you can do to make this difference even greater, which will lead people to say: "How do you do that without feeling nervous?"

2.1.3 Controlling those nerves

Remember, you *should* feel nervous if you want to do your best. The task is to *control* those nerves: they're still there but they perform a positive function rather than turning you into a state of collapse.

You may already have your own way of tackling frightening situations. If it works, by all means use it for tackling the apprehension of making a presentation. If you think that it may be a problem for you try the following:

 Think of people you know who you consider to be good at public speaking. Ask them:

- Whether or not they feel nervous about presenting.

- To give you any tips that they can for dealing with nerves.

About other people's tips: It's always worth finding out what you can learn from other people's experience. However:

- The answers you get may sometimes be contradictory.

- You may feel that some of the tips wouldn't work for you.

That is to be expected people are different, so what works for some may not work for others. So, always evaluate whether or not **you believe that it will work for you**. If you don't think it will work for you, don't try it. However, keep your notes: you may find that as you gain experience you will feel that you can try things that you would not have attempted earlier.

Note the answers you get in the tables on the next page. Put a tick in the right-hand box alongside the tips that you think are worth trying.

Number of speakers who said that they did feel nervous.	

Number of speakers who said that they did *not* feel nervous.	

Tips	✓

Some of the answers you got may well have been platitudes like:

'Don't worry', or even

'You've got nothing to worry about'.

These offer little or no help, so forget them! Who manages to stop worrying just because someone else told them not to?

A popular tip is:

Deep breathing, or a deep breath and count slowly to 10 immediately before you start to speak.

This makes sense because physiologically the deep breathing counteracts the responses engendered by the nerves.

Another suggestion you may have been given is:

'Think of your audience with no clothes on'.

This obviously works for some people: before trying it yourself make sure you are not overcome with laughter or dissolve into giggles.

The key is:

Find something that *fills* your mind.

Unless you do this, you will probably think of yourself. That thought is the *one most likely to increase* your nervousness. It is inevitable because your uppermost thought about yourself will be how you feel: nervous!

So, in evaluating the answers you have been given, consider how effective the tips would be in monopolising your thinking. Would they be powerful enough to:

•   Require your full concentration and prevent you thinking about yourself?

The closer you get to the start of your speech the worse the nerves become. So that's when it's most important to have your method of controlling those nerves.

My own method is to focus on the things that I should do to get off to the right start, for example:

- From where *exactly* should I start speaking?

- Check that the visual aid equipment is working.

- Will all the audience be able to see properly?

- Will I get in the way of anyone's view of the screen?

- Will I be able to make eye contact with everyone from where I've chosen to stand?

- Should I suggest that anyone moves: e.g. because their view may be obscured?

- Have I got anything in my pockets which might rattle and create a distraction?

- Are the pens still writing? Have any run dry?

It's true that, with good preparation, these should have been checked beforehand but a final confirmation is always worthwhile. For example, there may be a late arrival in the audience or the last speaker may have brushed the overhead projector as they finished and it's no longer focused on the screen.

It's also true that many of them are not essential for the presentation to be successful although each one helps. The more important points are that they:

- Occupy you both mentally and physically: make you too busy to think about yourself and how you feel.

- Focus your mind positively: get you thinking about things you are going to make happen. When you are going to make something happen you brush aside anything which gets in the way, in this case nerves!

- Give you a feeling of being in control: instead of just accepting what others have done, you are taking positive action to get things as you want them.

Another advantage is that the more you are able to do, the more the venue feels like *your* place and you begin to feel *at home* there. You should, therefore, try to:

- See the venue in advance if you are not familiar with it, and check the points listed in Appendix A, page 111.

- Arrive early on the day to check the points listed in Appendix B, page 112.

Even if you are following another speaker, be prepared to make changes if you feel that this will be better for your presentation. Aim to take no more than a minute or two. Work out what you want to do in advance and warn the audience about how long it will take: they can then use the time as they want rather than sit and watch your every move.

Showing that you are in control can also impress the audience before you've said a word.

It really does work. I always stress the importance of checking how the equipment you will be using operates. Following one course I ran, a delegate, who was to give a presentation to two hundred senior executives, called with a story proving this. Apparently the previous speaker had had a problem during his presentation because he couldn't find out how to switch on the overhead projector. The delegate had checked, however, beforehand so he was able to come to the rescue. In doing so, he boosted his confidence for the start of his presentation and conveyed to the audience: "Here's somebody who knows what they're doing, they will be worth listening to."

Making nerves work for you

Keynotes

- Feeling nervous is necessary if you are to do your best, (**2.1.1**, p 16).

- The secret is not to appear nervous, although you are, (**2.1.1**, p 17).

- Remember W Y F I *N* W O S – you usually look better than you feel, (**2.1.2**, p 17).

The secret of controlling nerves is to:

- Find something to fill your mind, (**2.1.3**, p 20).

- Focus your mind positively, on things you are going to make happen, (**2.1.3**, p 21).

- Take control instead of waiting for things to happen to you, (**2.1.3**, p 21).

2.2 Projecting confidence

So, you've tackled those nerves and got started. What might get in the way and indicate to the audience that you really do feel nervous? Let's go back to being in the audience and think about this.

 When you've been in an audience, what has the presenter done which suggested to you that they were nervous? Note your points in the frame below.

Indicators of nervousness

2.2.1 Three don'ts and how to avoid them

Some of your answers will relate to forgetting their lines, stuttering etc. Much of this can be avoided by preparing properly; we will consider what is involved in Sections 3, 4 and 5.

Many of your answers probably come under the headings of three major 'don'ts':

- Fiddling (e.g. with necklace, sleeve, hair)

- Playing with something in their hand (notes, pen, pencil, pointer etc.)

- Monotonous movement (e.g. sway, repetitive hand gesture).

And what effect did the presenter's apparent nervousness have on you? Their discomfort tends to make their audience feel uncomfortable too. At best, it gets in the way of the message the presenter is trying to convey. More seriously, it may undermine the audience's confidence in the presenter and their credibility. Let's look at what you can do to avoid these 'don'ts'.

Fiddling with clothing

This often arises because of discomfort, such as:

- Long sleeve which you feel needs to be pushed back continually;

- Tight collar which threatens to choke you;

- Tie or necklace which just will not stay in the right place;

- Hair which keeps falling over your face.

I've seen professionals caught out by something like this and have to change for the second part of their show. To avoid these problems:

Make sure that you feel comfortable for the presentation.

Physical comfort is only one important aspect of what you choose to wear. Your grooming and clothes are basic ingredients of the image you project to the audience. They are part of the first impression you create: the audience makes inferences from them about your self-image and your approach to the presentation. This can be from 'you look sloppy and couldn't be bothered' to 'you look smart and have taken care'.

So, choose clothing which you:

- Feel good about;

- Think will create a positive impression on the audience.

Playing with something

Did you include this on your list? The audience will see it as nervousness, rightly or wrongly. Even if they don't, they are likely to be distracted.

In fact, it may not be nervousness. How long do people hold something in their hand, which they are not using, before they start playing with it?

Usually a very short time, seldom more than a minute. If you have something in your hand, e.g. a pencil, pen, pointer, which you are not using, it is *natural* to fiddle with it. You are also unlikely to realise that you are doing it.

Of course, there will be times when you will need to have things in your hand during a presentation. When you do:

> Develop the habit of putting things down as soon as you have finished using them.

Monotonous movement

Your list of signs of nervousness probably included distracting movement. Certainly movement can be very distracting for the audience and is often a sign of nerves. This has led to one of the myths of good presentation that has been passed on over the years: keep still during your presentation.

It is this myth that is *the cause* of much distracting movement. Very few people naturally remain still when they are communicating, so if they try to do so, they are attempting something which does not come naturally to them.

The items on your list are probably repetitive movements; it is the repetition which makes them distracting. When I first learned presentation I was instructed that I must anchor my feet to the floor. Let's consider what happens if you try to follow this advice.

1.   The need to anchor your feet to the floor gets firmly fixed in your mind.

2.   By keeping this message in the forefront of your mind, you manage to keep your feet anchored to the floor.

3.   It is, however, unnatural to remain completely still. The compromise is to sway: your feet are still anchored to the floor but now there is some movement of your body over your anchored feet .

4.   Worse may be to come: after time the sway increases and you feel that you may topple over. So the feet no longer remain anchored to the floor: you shuffle from side to side as your weight shifts from one foot to another. You have started *the speaker's dance*. All because you tried to do the unnatural, i.e. remain still!

So, ignore the myth. Instead ensure that the movement which is part of your normal communication is carried through when you are presenting.

> The best way of avoiding unnatural movement is to ensure that you move as you would do naturally.

For example, people often ask what to do with their hands when they are presenting. The answer is: what you would do normally when you are communicating. Certainly this is much more for some people than others and you need to find out what is natural for you.

Since it is natural, you do it unconsciously and may not know what this movement is. I have often had people on a course protesting that they do not move when they communicate as they gesticulate vigorously to make their point!

When it is really working in a presentation you won't have to think about what to do with your hands. You will use them as you would do normally and will be similarly unaware of what you did. The message is:

Be yourself

You can play that role far more effectively than any other.

You may need to find out more about what you do normally if you are to *Be Yourself* when you present.

Ask some people who know you well:

- What movements they have noticed you make when communicating

- How these movements affect them, if at all.

Note your answers in the table on the next page. For any movement which they suggest has a negative effect, put a cross in the negative effect column.

My communication movements	Negative effect?

Check for yourself what you do in different situations, to see if they are right.

This personal research may highlight that you have mannerisms which have become part of you. The question is: do they matter? (Hence asking about their effect.) It may be that most people have come to accept them as part of you. They can even be an advantage with people, as they are seen as rather endearing. In this case it is probably better to leave them alone even if some people are irritated by them.

Would David Bellamy be a better presenter if he had his hands tied behind his back or would this stop his natural enthusiasm?

If you do have any mannerisms which are having a negative effect, it will not work to try and eradicate them *only* when giving a presentation. You will be trying to impose something on yourself which is unnatural to you: this will make you feel uncomfortable and you will not *Be Yourself.* You need to decide whether or not you want to change them for *all your communication* activities. If you make the change in what you do when communicating generally, this will follow through naturally into your presentation. It won't be easy and it will require patience.

Now put a second cross in the negative effect column beside any point that *you* feel you want to do something about for all your communication activities.

Decide how you are going to try and deal with them:

• Are you going to rely on spotting for yourself when you are using them?

• Do you know some people who could help by noting when you are using them and telling you?

2.3 The PLUS factor

So, you have overcome the nerves, got started and are making your presentation confidently and naturally without distractions. Is this enough?

Unfortunately, no.

2.3.1 Presentation not conversation

Normal delivery is fine for everyday conversation but it is not going to keep your audience listening for that longer period of time which is necessary for you to achieve your purpose.

If you are to succeed in that you will have to get:

> *All* of your audience to *continue to listen* until you have presented *all* the points you need to make.

This will usually take rather longer than a minute or two which is the most that is required in normal conversation or at a meeting.

How often have you been in an audience and witnessed the following?

- The speaker is presenting with little or no animation and starts to lose their audience
- The audience, particularly those toward the back, start to shuffle
- The speaker, probably belatedly, notices that they have lost the attention of their audience
- The speaker asks the audience whether or not they can hear!
- The audience answer that they cannot hear!

You may wonder how they managed to answer the question if they could not hear, but few see anything unusual when this happens. In fact, the audience is telling the speaker that their attention is not being held rather than that they cannot hear.

The sequel is usually that the speaker speaks up, *for a little while*, then lapses back into an ineffective delivery – which they believe to be sufficient.

This highlights that there is a difference between what the speaker *thinks* is necessary, and what *actually* is necessary to hold the audience's attention.

Your normal delivery is not enough and we need to modify *Be Yourself* into:

Be Super You

2.3.2 *Super You*

Both words are critical:

- **Super** because achieving your best means pushing yourself to the limits of being you

- **You** because you are not trying to be someone else – we have already said that the role you play best is yourself.

Let's think about somebody doing something to the best of their ability where we can measure how successful they have been. For example, it may be running 1500 metres, throwing the javelin or doing the triple jump.

If they are successful in achieving a result which is better than they have managed before, they will be elated and tired, if not exhausted, with the effort they have made. They have had to push themselves to the limit to get the result – they have been their *Super Self*.

Presenting is another example of using your skills. So extra effort is necessary to get the best results from your presentations.

If you just talk as you do normally, you cannot expect to hold attention for longer than you would do if you were having a conversation with them i.e. a minute or two. You are, therefore, going to have to do something which you have a lot of experience of, but do it differently.

SUPER YOU = YOURSELF + THE PLUS FACTOR

That difference will make it feel odd to you because it means:

> Presenting in a way which seems, *to you*, to be exaggerated.

It will seem exaggerated to you only because you are doing something you are used to doing, but in a different way.

Think of your experiences of trying to change the way you do something which has become a habit, e.g. turning yourself from a two-finger typist to one who uses both hands. When you first try to change, it feels awful and initially, your proficiency probably gets worse. However, if you are prepared to persevere you get the benefits of better performance.

What is the form of this exaggeration in your presentation?

> Overemphasis in your movement –
>
> e.g. stronger hand gestures
>
>
> Overemphasis in your voice –
>
> louder and with greater variation than you think is necessary.

Although it will seem to be exaggerated to you, *it must not appear that way to your audience.*

2.3.3 Knowing *Super You*

We now have two ends of a spectrum: normal conversation and the ultimate *Super You*, the maximum you can achieve without appearing to be exaggerated.

How do you get it right? The first step is to think about what happens when you communicate normally and get feedback from people who you know well and can trust.

Let us consider your normal communication first. Remember, we have seen that if you want to make a change you should try to do this in your communication generally, not just in your presentations.

 Answer the questions below in relation to your normal communication, not specifically to any presenting which you have already done.

1. How often have you been told you speak too loudly? What were the circumstances, e.g. was it when others wanted to be quiet?

2. How often do others say they haven't heard what you said?

3. How often have you been asked to speak up?

4. How would you describe your voice?

5. And how do others describe it? Ask them if you don't know.

6. When you are enthusiastic about something, how does this come across to others?

7.   Which of the following best describes you?

Other people say I always come across with charisma.	
I usually manage to project enthusiasm.	
I sometimes convey enthusiasm, but it's hard work.	
I can be enthusiastic but only when I really like the subject.	
I have great difficulty in conveying enthusiasm	
I just can't show enthusiasm, it's not me!	

Many people think that if someone has charisma it's something they were born with. Conversely, if you weren't born with it there's nothing you can do about it. There *may* be *some* truth in this, but it's certainly not the full story.

How do you know whether or not someone is charismatic? Have you seen people who might be regarded as charismatic failing to enthuse their audience? And have you also seen many people who wouldn't normally be considered to be charismatic inspire an audience?

You can't see charisma. You can only see people behaving in a charismatic way, or being **Super You**. Everyone is capable of displaying charisma, when they are sufficiently motivated to do so.

Try preparing a short talk and:

Either speak it out loud and record it on video;

or deliver it to a group of trusted friends (also try to video it if you can).

- Have a look at it and/or get the reaction of those trusted friends. How would you, and they, rate it on the following scale?

0	25	50	70	90	100	110
Boring	Moderately interesting	Average	Good, could be even better	Nearly there	Your best	Over the top

- Would it have been better if it had been more animated? If so, try again, with more animation. You can repeat this until you are satisfied or until you and those friends have had enough!

2.4 Keeping them listening

We've already seen that keeping people's attention is a key issue for the presenter. Even if the presenter does project confidence and use the plus factor there is a limit to how long they will keep their audience listening. The typical picture for a presenter speaking to a group of people is shown in the graph below.

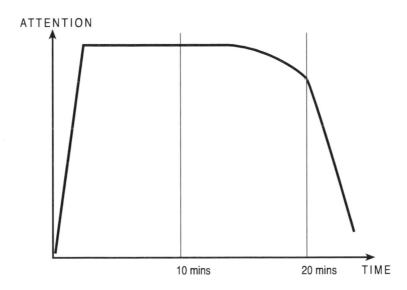

2.4.1 The 20-minute rule

> Don't attempt to continue speaking for more than 20 minutes at a time.

Of course the actual time before that steep descent will depend on factors such as the time of day, the audience's interest in the subject, how well it is presented and the temperature and stuffiness of the room. It does not take them long to decide that a presentation is not worth listening to, for example because they think the presenter does not know what they are talking about.

The attention from the audience is much more likely to go into steep decline before the 20 minutes is up, rather than the presenter managing to hold their attention for longer than this. Research also shows that our attention span is getting shorter. In summary:

- If you carry on talking for more than 20 minutes without a break, all you do is interfere with what you have just achieved;

- It is better to present for no more than 10–15 minutes at a time.

You have probably experienced the presenter who *had* to carry on until they had finished, regardless of the 20-minute rule. But with what result?

- The audience's attention begins to drift, although, at first, there may be no obvious sign that they are no longer listening.

- Then they start to show signs: shifting in their seats, etc.

- If this has no effect their loss of attention may well become irritation with the presenter.

So what do you do if what you have to present is going to take longer than this?

> **Give them a break!**

This does not literally mean stopping for tea or coffee or giving them the chance to get rid of the tea/coffee that they have already had! You have between an hour and an hour and a half before this type of break is necessary.

What is needed is to give them a change from sitting and listening passively to you. Get them to take a more active part, for example:

- Give them a chance to ask questions, either as you go along or by stopping at specific points

- Buzz groups: organise them into small groups of three to six people, and ask them to discuss their ideas on a particular point for up to five minutes.

Following the 20-minute rule does not mean that you will keep them listening. It simply ensures that you don't attempt the impossible.

Circumstances are both:

- Within your control – how well you present, and

- Outside your control – environmental factors, ventilation etc.

Let us look at the circumstances that are within your control. *Super You* is presenting confidently with the plus factor; is there anything else you can do?

Let's go back to your experience in an audience:

What techniques have you seen a presenter successfully use to attract the audience's attention and keep them listening during their presentation? Examples can be how they have interacted with their audience, or things they have done to make the content more interesting. Make a note in the box on the next page.

Attracting the audience's attention/keeping them listening

We will consider these techniques under two main headings:

- Interacting with the audience
- Making the content more interesting.

2.4.2 Interacting with the audience

Geography: the way things are set up for your presentation can encourage or discourage interaction, both in the minds of the audience and the presenter. The presenter discourages interaction if they distance themselves from their audience, either by standing apart, or by remaining fixed behind a barrier, lectern or table.

Avoid alienation: think about your audience and what is acceptable/unacceptable to them. Inappropriate dress is one example of alienation, see Section 2.2.1, page 25; others are political incorrectness, jargon and the wrong use of humour.

Two-way: questions are one method of making the presentation two-way. Obviously interaction is better if you are prepared to take questions as you go along, but this is more difficult to control. You can also encourage interaction by asking questions to stimulate discussion, or by using the rhetorical question to get them to answer in their own minds.

Activity: questions are an example of this. You can also ask for a show of hands, or ask them to write something down, or discuss something in buzz groups, or ask them to think about a particular point and pause to give them the chance to do so etc.

Smile: this helps the audience warm to you. Most people relate to somebody who is looking cheerful, rather than someone who looks glum. However:

- Remember the maxim: *Be yourself.* It is counterproductive to pin an unnatural smile on you face because it will probably be misinterpreted.

- There are times when it is inappropriate to smile, for example an undertaker addressing the bereaved.

If it is appropriate, try thinking of something which amuses you before you start, so you can smile to get yourself in the right frame of mind.

Eye contact: the presenter who looks at the floor or ceiling will soon lose contact with their audience and loss of their attention will quickly follow. Eye contact conveys to the audience that you are interested in them it also makes them more alert to staying with you.

Eye contact must be with *all* the audience. There is a temptation to focus on one person who is obviously agreeing with you. Resist it – you may be missing the opportunity to spot that you are losing the others.

If you are speaking to hundreds of people you cannot have eye contact with each one of them. In this case, you scan around the audience looking just above them. If you notice a movement you can stop at that person to see what it signifies.

Eye contact signifies to the audience that you are interested in them. At the same time you get feedback: their body language conveys whether or not they are following you, are puzzled, or agree, disagree or are losing interest.

 Body language is something we tend to respond to without thinking about it. Let's consider what you already know and use. Try filling in the table on this and the next page:

- In the left-hand column, note all the body language you perceive as positive under the relevant subheading, e.g. *facial* and *head*.

- In the right-hand column, note all the body language you perceive as negative under the relevant subheading, e.g. *facial* and *head*.

Positive signals	Negative signals
Facial	
Head	

Positive signals	Negative signals
Hands and arms	
Legs and feet	
Posture and body orientation	

The table below identifies body language 'gestures' which tend to be positive and those which tend to be negative.

Positive signals	Negative signals
Facial	
Active eye contact Smile	Unblinking eyes Looking away Down-tilted eyebrows Wrinkled nose Nervous lip licking Tight lips
Head	
Tilted slightly in listening position Nodding	Yawning
Hands and arms	
Open movements One/both hands touching face	Arms folded Palm to back of neck Hands clenched Drumming on table Head in hands Doodling Hand over mouth when speaking Rubbing/touching nose
Legs and feet	
Uncrossed legs Feet on tiptoe	Legs crossed Feet flat on floor Feet tapping
Posture and body orientation	
Sitting forward Sitting on edge of seat	Body turned away Shuffling when asked questions Talking to someone else

Body language is not an exact science. Picking out one particular piece of body language, e.g.: arms folded, can be misleading. For this reason, it should be:

- Considered for its *congruence* with other gestures etc.

- Interpreted in *clusters*, i.e. several different gestures, rather than focusing on one only.

Your awareness can be developed through practice. Until you feel really confident in your ability to interpret body language accurately, it is best to regard it as a clue. So, if the gestures appear to be negative, use that as a signal to check it out, for example, with a question. See Appendix C, page 113, for further reading on Body Language.

2.4.3 Making the content more interesting

Personalise: this takes us back to thinking about the audience. It is useful, for example, to use individuals' names and refer to group interests within the audience, provided that this is done genuinely.

Keep it digestible: the 20-minute rule applies to attention in terms of time. The amount covered is also critical. People normally take in no more than seven points before they need a break to absorb them. As with the 20-minute rule, this maximum may well be reduced if the points are relatively complex.

Use of stories/examples: these help to bring your presentation to life. They are also useful to help reinforce important points to the audience.

Humour: undoubtedly this can help to keep people listening, if it works. It can be devastating if it does not work. So, apply the maxim: *if in doubt, don't*. The doubt may be, for example, whether or not the audience will find it acceptable or whether or not they will laugh if *you* tell it. A safer way of introducing humour is to use a story which is relevant and acceptable; it does not matter whether or not they laugh because it is relevant but if they do it is a bonus.

Suspense: all the best soaps end up with a *what will happen next* situation. That is one of the ways they keep people watching. Similarly, you can introduce the *what's coming next* idea as a way to encourage the audience to listen to your presentation.

Visual aids: the sense of vision is the most active in receiving and absorbing information. So it is important to make sure you are giving it something to do if you want to keep attention.

Powerful presenting

Keynotes

Projecting confidence

- Before you start, make, sure you will feel comfortable and will project a positive image, (**2.2.1**, p 25).

- If you pick something up, put it down *as soon as* you have finished using it, (**2.2.1**, p 26).

- Be yourself: moving naturally is the best way to avoid distracting movement, (**2.2.1**, pp 27/28).

The PLUS factor

- Holding attention for a presentation requires much more effort than for a conversation, (**2.3.1**, p 29).

- Super You = yourself + the plus factor: it may seem odd to you but it is how it comes across to your audience that matters, (**2.3.2**, pp 30/31).

Keeping them listening

- Remember the 20-minute rule; use breaks if you need to take longer, (**2.4.1**, pp 33/34).

- Keep attention by interacting with your audience – how you set it up, making it two-way etc., (**2.4.2**, p 36).

- Maintain eye contact around all the audience because that way you get feedback from their body language, (**2.4.2**, pp 36/37).

- Add interest to the content by personalising, using stories etc., (**2.4.3**, p 40).

3

The Strategy
for Success

3.0 Introduction

3.1 Identify the purpose

3.2 Specify the audience

3.3 Test for success

3.4 The PLY approach

3.0 Introduction

Getting and keeping attention is partly a matter of how well the presenter puts their content across. But a presentation, however powerful, will *not* succeed unless the content is right; this cannot happen on the spur of the moment. Even though a good presentation may appear to be spontaneous, it is only good as a result of careful preparation.

So, where do we start? All too often, our first thought when called upon to give a presentation is about the content: *What can I talk about?*

In fact, if you want to get the content right, it is *not* the first thing to think about.

 Think of a situation where you were successful in persuading a friend or colleague to do something when you thought they might not agree. What did you do before you went to speak to them?

How you prepared to persuade your friend or colleague ☺

You knew what you wanted to achieve and you knew your audience. So, to improve your chance of persuading them you were able to think about:

- Whether or not you thought they would agree;

- Why *they* might want to do what you were going to suggest;

- How you would approach issues which they might find sensitive;

- The objections they might raise and how you would answer them.

However, in these one-to-one situations you have more chance to adjust what you do according to the circumstances. You may, for example, decide that now is not the best time to try and persuade them because they are in a bad mood or are preoccupied. So you leave it until later.

In this section of the workbook we will assume that you do not have this flexibility. You are going to have to give a presentation at a specified time to a specific group of people. Because of the reduced flexibility you will have to plan more rigorously if you are to succeed.

The first thing is to work out your strategy, which involves four steps:

1. Be clear about what you want to achieve.

   See Section 3.1: **Identify the purpose.**

2. Know precisely who you are talking to.

   See Section 3.2: **Specify the audience.**

3. Ensure that what you want to achieve from the presentation is reasonable.

   See Section 3.3: **Test for success.**

4. Match your content to your audience.

   See Section 3.4: **The PLY approach.**

You probably go through these steps quite frequently without realising it. We have seen that they should be considered in any situation where you are communicating with a purpose; for example, persuading a friend or colleague to do something, or at an interview.

3.1 Identify the purpose

Why are you giving this presentation? The first answer to this question may be:

- My boss has told me to

- It is my turn

- They couldn't find anyone else

- I couldn't find anyone else.

That may be true, but it does not move us forward. Let us look at your thoughts.

 Why might people give a presentation, apart from the fact that they cannot avoid it?

Note your answers in the frame below.

```
┌─────────────────────────────────────────────────────────────────┐
│  Purposes of presentation                                         │
│                                                                   │
│                                                                   │
│                                                                   │
│                                                                   │
│                                                                   │
│                                                                   │
│                                                                   │
│                                                                   │
│                                                                   │
│                                                                   │
│                                                                   │
│                                                                   │
│                                                                   │
│                                                                   │
└─────────────────────────────────────────────────────────────────┘
```

3.1.1 Why? – The end result

In answering the question why? it is vital to distinguish clearly between *what* you are going to do and *why* you are going to do it. Some possible answers are:

- To give instructions
- To make the audience aware
- To tell/inform
- To report on something.

The answers state *what's* going to happen in the presentation not *why* it is going to happen.

Just think what a presentation costs in terms of the time for those attending, the presenter's time, in preparation as well as delivery. And what about all that nervous energy the presenter generates? All this is wasted unless the presentation leads to something positive as a result, an *end result.* This may be:

- An action which is to be taken
- A change in the way the audience feel about something, for example being more motivated.

What the presenter is going to do, for example to inform, is not a positive end result. It is the means used to achieve the end. The key is *why* the presenter is going to inform – if there's no purpose, why bother? The *end result* is what makes the effort involved worth it.

So, the question you need to answer about **why?** is:

What end result is to be achieved?

Giving a presentation is like a journey. The first decision is to determine your destination. So, think about the *end result* you want to reach and how you will measure the success of your presentation, i.e. know when you have reached your destination.

Now go back to your list of purposes on the previous page. Tick those which are end results, for example:

- to sell a product;
- to get a recommendation accepted;
- to persuade the audience that an idea should be implemented;
- to enable the audience to perform a particular task;
- to convince that you are getting on satisfactorily and no interference is needed;
- to motivate to tackle a task enthusiastically;
- to encourage the audience to tell other people about your idea/product/organisation.

3.1.2 Presentation or training?

Let us look at why it is so important to answer the **why?** There are two basic reasons for giving a presentation:

- **Persuasion:** getting people to do something that they would *not do* without the presentation this includes selling, getting approval, inspiring and motivating.

- **Training:** enabling people to do something that they would *not be able to do* without the presentation.

 Both require the use of good presentation skills, but otherwise they are very different. The table below shows some statements about a presentation given to train and some incomplete statements about a presentation given to persuade. Try completing the statements about persuasion.

Training	Persuasion
Could **not** do what is wanted before being trained.	Could _____
Change needed in the audience's *ability* to do something.	Change needed in _____
If the purpose is to be achieved, the presentation must help the audience to attain the knowledge and/or skill needed to do what is wanted.	If the purpose is to be achieved the presentation must _____
Need to remember most, if not all, of the content after the training.	Need to remember _____
Next step is for the audience to go away and do what is required correctly.	Next step is _____

With persuasion:

- They *could* agree before the presentation but *probably* would not do so. If they would, you probably don't need to give the presentation.

- Change needed in whether or not the audience are *prepared* to do something.

- If the purpose is to be achieved, the presentation must convince the audience through logical argument and/or changing their feelings.

- They need to remember little of the content after the presentation.

- Next step is to agree on the course of action as a result of the agreement.

For example, your boss has asked you to give a presentation to the Management Committee on an idea you want them to take up.

- They could agree just as a result of you making the suggestion. However, they will probably need to be convinced first.

- To achieve what you want, you have to change whether or not they are prepared to agree.

- So, the purpose of your presentation is to convince them that this action should be taken and/or overcome any doubts they may have.

- If they agree all you need them to remember is that they did so. They don't have to remember the detail of your argument. You could put this in writing if needed.

- The next step is to agree who is to do what.

Persuasion and training involve bringing about a change in your audience, but the nature of the change differs markedly. So, your presentation style will be very different, depending on whether you are persuading or training. If you are training, you will need to help them if they are to remember the content later, for example by repetition and/or opportunity to practise.

Presentations sometimes involve elements of persuading and training. This added complication means that your success depends on answering:

- Which points will your audience have to be persuaded about?

- Which do they have to learn to be able to do?

- Which comes first?

Your purpose is now clear but achieving it involves other people, your audience. So now you need to think about who they are.

3.2 Specify the audience

The bespoke tailor gets business, their end result, by making clothes especially to fit the person they are making them for. They take considerable care measuring their customers to ensure that the clothes fit; their business depends on it.

If you are to achieve *your* end result, you will have to bring about changes in your audience. You will be successful only if you make your presentation bespoke for them. If you are to do this you need to be able to:

> Look at the presentati*on through the eyes of your audience.

Unless you *deliberately* think how it will look from the audience's viewpoint, you will be seeing it from your angle. Can you see from their point of view why *your* end result is to *their* advantage? You won't be able to, unless you understand how they see it.

> The art of persuasion is to show other people why something is to their advantage.

So looking at it from their point of view:

- What are their needs?
- What problems do they have that you might help to solve?
- How will the end result be to their advantage?
- What are the disadvantages, if any?

They will be posing the crunch question:

> **WIIFM?**
>
> **What's in it for me?**

They may not ask it outright, but your success depends on answering it to *their* satisfaction.

I Hate Giving Presentations! published by Fenman Ltd © 1997 Michael D. Owen

What should you know about your audience so that you can look at the presentation through their eyes and show them why your end result is to their advantage? Note your thoughts in the frame below.

The audience

As with the successful tailor, you have to get a lot of information in order to answer:

3.2.1 Who? – specifically

Expectations

- What are they expecting from the presentation?

They will have their expectations, positive or negative, they may be expecting to be interested or bored. This may depend, for example, on their interest in the subject, their previous experience of presentations on the topic, or on their expectations of you.

Knowledge and experience

- How much do they know at the moment?
- What technical language and jargon do they know/not know?

You must know the answers so that you can decide the level at which you should pitch what you are going to say.

Background

- What type of people are they?

Some people may accept points backed by only limited factual evidence, particularly if the presentation has polish. However, people with an analytical background (scientists, technicians, bankers, etc.) have been trained to expect factual detail and are unlikely to be convinced without it.

You and them

- What is your credibility with them?

If they know you already, they will have a perception of your position in relation to theirs and of your expertise.

Opinions

- What preconceived opinions do they have on the topic?

Opinions are formed on the basis of information. What evidence have they used to form their opinions, and is it correct?

Attitudes and feelings

There may be an overlap between attitudes, feelings and opinions; there is also an important difference. Attitudes and feelings have an emotional base and are seldom changed by rational argument.

- What is their attitude?

- What preconceived feelings do they have, e.g. prejudices, politics or fear?

Decision making

If persuasion is your end result:

- How does the group reach their decisions?

- If it is by consensus, who are the main influencers?

- Are you speaking to the person(s) with the authority to agree?

If training is your end result:

- How are they going to implement it?

Problems

It is advisable to assume that you will have to overcome some hurdles if you are to be successful. You will be very lucky if you avoid them, and you will find it much easier to deal with them if you have thought about them in advance.

- What awkward questions might they ask?

- What objections might they raise?

- What interpersonal problems might you have to deal with (for example, people who don't get on with each other, or with you)?

3.2.2 Getting the information

So, there's a lot you should know about the audience. Because it is often not easy to get the information, many presenters tend to try and get away without bothering. This is dangerous. Missing information can lead you to unknowingly getting the presentation wrong for that audience, for example:

- Assuming they know something which they don't, and losing them.

- Not being prepared to answer a question which they believe to be important.

- Failing to anticipate a negative attitude.

This can end up being as unsuccessful as the tailor who has made the perfect suit except that the sleeves are too long. At least they have the chance to put it right.

The presenter often does not get this second chance.

Do all you reasonably can to minimise the uncertainty. Think about what you
know already, who else may be able to give help; possibly even contacting some
of those who will be coming and what's available from research, e.g. the database.
Remember your success depends on you:

> # Changing the audience from
> ## *How they see it now* to
> ## *How they will have to see it*
> ## *if* they are to commit themselves to
> ## *your* end result.

3.3 Test for success

Judy Turner, IT Director of Wonderland Plc, has been asked by the Executive Committee to investigate the latest *Whizzo* Computer and give a presentation at its next meeting. Her research has convinced her that Wonderland should purchase *Whizzo*, but, because it is so good, it is very expensive. The company's financial situation is tough and Tony Block, Finance Director, supported by Len Back, Company Secretary, has got the Committee to defer several purchases recently. Other committee members have lost out as a result.

Judy knows that *Whizzo* would provide the opportunity to access the very latest programmes. These will give major, but different, benefits to Tony Block, Sarah Moresell (Sales and Marketing Director) and Charlie Makepiece (Production Director). A further problem is that Fred Slocombe, Human Resources Director, will be worried about the potential personnel problems and does not really understand computers. Unfortunately there will be no opportunity to speak to any of them before the meeting.

What should she do?

3.3.1 The realistic test

Judy has to consider several facts:

- The current climate is against new purchases

- Tony Block will be opposed

- He will be supported by Len Back

- Sarah Moresell and Charlie Makepiece have had purchase requests deferred and will probably be opposed to the idea unless they can see strong benefits for themselves

- Strong benefits do exist for them, and for Tony Block, but they are different for the three Directors

- Fred Slocombe will also be opposed, for the wrong reasons.

If Judy tries to explain the benefits during the presentation, only the one person concerned is going to be interested while she is doing so. She also needs to speak to Fred Slocombe about his concerns.

The obvious thing to do is to see them individually, but she cannot do so before the meeting.

Judy now applies **The Realistic Test**:

> ## THE REALISTIC TEST
>
> Is your end result **realistic** bearing in mind the audience and
> time available?

Judy's answer is *no*. She is convinced that Wonderland Plc should purchase *Whizzo* but does not believe that she will get the Committee to agree.

She must, therefore, modify the *end result* for her presentation. It becomes: to get the Executive Committee to agree that she should discuss the details with Tony Block, Sarah Moresell, Charlie Makepiece and Fred Slocombe and then decide at the next meeting.

What she wants to eventually achieve does *not* change. She still wants to get the Committee to agree to purchase *Whizzo*. But, because she does not believe this is possible as a result of this presentation, it now becomes her *ultimate aim*.

If your answer to the realistic test is *yes*:

- Your presentation *end result* does *not* need to be changed.

If it is *no*:

- Your original end result becomes your *ultimate aim*.

- Your presentation becomes a step towards your *ultimate aim*.

- Your new *end result* for your presentation is a realistic positive step towards your *ultimate aim*.

3.3.2 End result and ultimate aim

Here are further examples to demonstrate the difference between the two:

Any parent with teenage children knows that they are well aware of the *realistic test*. Their *end result* starts with a new pair of jeans; the current ones are badly tattered so that's reasonable. Then the footwear looks dreadful with the new jeans etc., until their *ultimate aim* of a new outfit is achieved. Would you have agreed to the new outfit if that's what they had asked for originally?

The Telesales Manager's ultimate aim might be that a member of telephone sales staff could serve a customer without referring to notes. However, training would take a lot longer if they were not allowed to refer to notes while they were still learning. They might decide to accept an *end result* of doing the job referring to notes, knowing that their *ultimate aim*, i.e. doing it without notes, would be achieved once they had got some experience.

What factors affect whether an end result needs to be modified because the ultimate aim could not be achieved by the presentation? Note your answers in the frame below.

Factors affecting the achievement of your ultimate aim

I Hate Giving Presentations! published by Fenman Ltd © 1997 Michael D. Owen

Factors to consider include:

What can you realistically expect the audience to commit themselves to immediately?

For example, if you try to persuade the Board to spend a lot of money they may not be prepared to agree straight away. They may want to go away and think about it before making a commitment. Trying to push them too far could stimulate resistance and lead to failure. This was a problem for Judy Turner in our example (page 54).

How easy will it be to achieve your end result?

If you want the audience to make a big change you may expect too much If you try to achieve this in one step. You may need to do it in two, or even more, steps if you are to be successful. This is particularly true when emotions or attitude changes are involved. You can be direct if they are 'with you', but will need to tackle issues much more sensitively when they may be negative, and this will take longer.

What depth will you need to cover to achieve your end result and how long have you got?

Frequently presenters fail to realise just how long it will take to present the content that they need to include. They then find that they cannot complete their presentation, they overrun, or rush through the last, often important, points. They then wonder why they did not succeed!

Is the audience starting with the same interest and knowledge?

If there are very different levels of knowledge or different interests in the audience it is often better, if possible, to give more than one presentation. It may be the only way to avoid losing some of them because they cannot understand or because they are bored!

What group dynamics problems might you have to overcome to achieve your aim?

For example, handling those people who automatically disagree with each other and the time it is going to take.

What is your credibility with the audience?

Do they see you as an authority before you start, or do you have to establish this? Do they see you as objective or as having a vested interest?

Are presentations being given by other people at the same time?

If so, you will need to find out what they are going to cover to avoid duplication, etc.

3.3.3 Do you need a package?

The presentation may sometimes be only part of what is necessary to achieve your ultimate aim. It must always, however, have an end result, even if for that eventual success you may need to put together a package of activities: before, during and after the presentation. At this stage, particularly if your analysis of the audience highlighted potential problems, you should think about:

Before your presentation

What can you do beforehand to improve your chance of success? For example:

- Go to see some people

- Speak to them on the phone

- Send them something to read.

If you try the last method, be sure that they are going to read it. Otherwise you can be in a worse position because some have read it thoroughly, some have skimmed through it, and the rest have not looked at it.

  Imagine you are going to have to give a presentation on a subject you know well. Decide on an imaginary audience, the time allocated and the purpose of your presentation. For example:

Subject	Your favourite soap
Audience (Who)	People who do not watch it
Time	20 minutes, including questions
Purpose	To persuade them to watch the next episode

Other possibilities for your subject are your hobby, or your favourite book.

In the table below note the information for your imaginary presentation.

Subject
Audience (Who)
Time
Purpose

Does this pass the realistic test?

3.4 The PLY approach

You have defined your purpose, specified your audience and tested for success. Now you can turn your attention to the content. If your content is going to be successful in achieving the end result, it must satisfy three criteria:

- *Positive* focus

- *Logical* . . . to your audience

- The *You* feeling.

3.4.1 *Positive* focus

Bad news is not positive, but that does not mean you should cover it up. Indeed, it is usually advisable to state it openly. If you are seen to be evasive, your credibility will be demolished and your chance of success ruined.

At the same time, recognise that your audience will be quickly put off by negatives, so bring them solutions, not problems:

- Ensure you counteract the negatives, e.g. by telling them what can be, or preferably *has been*, done to deal with the situation.

- Warn them of potential dangers but show how these can be avoided or overcome.

- If training, concentrate on what they should do, not what they should not do.

Another aspect of being positive is to avoid infamous remarks such as "Unaccustomed as I am to public speaking". They have a negative effect on:

- The audience – because they convey that your presentation may not be very good;

- You – because they remind you of your discomfort.

3.4.2 *Logical* . . . to your audience

Occasionally a presenter may deliberately say something which they believe is illogical, but which may have a particular purpose, e.g. to provoke discussion. Their intention should soon become clear to the audience.

As a member of an audience, what do you feel when you find it difficult to follow what the presenter is saying? Puzzled, dissatisfied, annoyed? However you feel, it is reasonable to assume that the presenter thought it was logical.

Theoretically, some may argue that logic is objective: what one person sees as logical, others will too. In practice this does not work. Many arguments arise because one person is convinced that something is logical whilst the other is not.

If a presentation is to be successful it is not the presenter's view that matters. If the audience is puzzled, dissatisfied or annoyed the presenter is unlikely to achieve their objective. So when preparing a presentation, you need to go back to looking at it through the eyes of the audience and answer:

> Will *the audience* see it as logical?

To help ensure that your presentation is logical to your audience, you must:

Relate the presentation to *their* knowledge and experience

- You have established your audience's knowledge and experience of the subject. Now you have to ensure that you build the bridge between this and any new information you wish to give.

- Depth: This will be influenced by their knowledge, experience and the type of people they are.

- Jargon: Will your listeners be familiar with it? If not, can you avoid using it?

- Statistics: If used, relate them to something familiar to your audience. Few people can comprehend what £1,000 million really means.

3.4.3 The *You* feeling

Think of the statement: "This afternoon I'm going to talk about . . ."

Who does this place the emphasis on? Not the audience, they don't even get a mention! If the presenter really had the audience in their mind when preparing, the words would have probably conveyed why the audience would be interested in listening.

You, meaning the audience, is the most important pronoun for the presenter. Build what you have to say around the pronouns you (the audience) and/or we, provided that it refers to both *you and your audience, not just your own organisation*.

So, instead of "I'm going to talk about . . ." use wording such as "This is particularly relevant to you because . . ." but make sure that you are right!

Using *you* follows naturally, if you have thought about the presentation from the audience's point of view. This also enables you to make the presentation come to life for your audience.

You may find the subject fascinating but will they? Yes, if you make it so. You may find the subject boring, but will they?

- *Yes*, if you look at it only from your point of view.

- *No*, if you find a way to arouse, and maintain, the audience's interest. That is your job. After all nobody likes to be a bore.

Remember: no subject is uninteresting – but the presenter can make it appear to be. Think of and use 'interest points', such as:

- Stories and anecdotes

- Case histories and examples

- Putting it another way

- Humour

- Visual aids.

Then there is one of the most important interest points of all, answering:

WIIFM? What's in it for me?

That is the crunch question which your audience is asking, and which you must answer if you want to succeed.

3.4.4 The PLY test

As you work on your content, you become absorbed in your thoughts. The more absorbed you get, the more you will tend unconsciously to look at it from your point of view – the *me* feeling. So, periodically you should stop and make a conscious effort to look at the content through the eyes of your audience. Does it pass the PLY test?

The PLY test

1. Will *the audience* find your presentation **Positive**?

2. Will *they* see it as **Logical**?

3. Does it have the **You** feeling?

The strategy for success

Keynotes

- The first step is *why* you are going to say it – what *end result* do you want to achieve? (**3.1.1**, p 46).

- Is your end result *persuading* them to agree or *training* them to do something they cannot do? (**3.1.2**, pp 47/48).

- Can you look at it through the eyes of your audience ? (**3.2,** p 49).

- Do you know enough about the audience to change them from *how they see it now* to *how they will have to see it*? (**3.2.2,** pp 52/53).

- Have you applied the *realistic test*? (**3.3.1**, pp 54/55).

- Have you considered the package which you need to get your ultimate aim, particularly whether you should do anything beforehand? (**3.3.3**, p 58).

- Are you using the PLY – Positive, Logical, You – approach? (**3.4**, pp 59/60).

4

The Structure for Success

4.0 Introduction

4.1 Conclusion

4.2 Developing the body

4.3 Attractive introduction

4.0 Introduction

In Section 3.1.2 (pages 47/48) we considered the difference between a presentation and training. The basic structure of both is introduction, body and conclusion, together with the opportunity for the audience to put their questions. However, there are differences in the content of these elements of the structure, so we will consider presentation and training separately.

4.0.1 The structure of a presentation

Introduction: to *sell* the presentation

You change the scene when you start to speak, so this is the easiest time to get the audience tuned in to listening to you. Your first task is to get their attention. Having done this you have to prove to them that your presentation is going to be a worthwhile experience for them.

In the introduction, the audience's crunch question *What's in it for me?* means:

* Why should I listen to you?

Body: to prove the case

Your introduction should have them wanting to listen to what you have to say, so now is the time to say it. The body of your presentation is where you put across the content required to achieve your end result. You have to keep them listening and lead them to that end result.

Here, their *What's in it for me?* means:

* Why do I need to change anything?
* Do the benefits, to me, of what you are proposing outweigh any inconvenience I may experience?

Conclusion: to lead to action

You use this to trigger the end result and underline the next step to be taken.

Their final *What's in it for me?* questions which you must answer to get their commitment are:

* Have you answered my reservations?
* Am I satisfied that the action you are proposing is both worthwhile and the best thing to do?

This is your content but to achieve your end result you will also have to answer:

Questions: to clear any obstacles

There will also need to be a chance for the audience to ask questions. You may choose to take these when the audience wants to ask them, or when you stop to take them. If you choose the latter, take them between the body and the conclusion.

The breakdown of the time to allocate for these different parts of the presentation is:

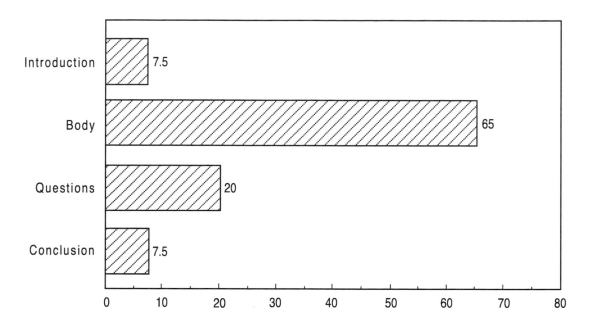

These are rough guidelines, not a precise statement of the breakdown. In a fifteen-minute presentation, this means one minute for the *introduction*, 10 minutes for the *body*, three minutes for *questions* and one minute for the *conclusion*.

4.0.2 Training: the similarities and the differences

We have seen that the end result of training is to enable people to do something that they would not be able to do without the training. Achieving this usually requires:

•   A presentation of information.

•   An opportunity for the learners to consolidate the information in their mind so that they remember it.

•   Further learning, e.g. of the necessary skills. Nobody will learn to drive merely by being told what to do!

This workbook does not attempt to go into the full complexities of effective training, in particular the further learning that may be an integral part of achieving the end result. However, the presentation of information to create learning may be part of achieving the end result. Everything in the workbook is relevant to this aspect of training but the structure needs to be modified:

Introduction: to sell the training

- You still have to get their attention, and

- Prove to them that the training is going to be a worthwhile experience for *them*.

Body: to create learning

- You have to keep them listening while you get them to absorb the content required to achieve your end result.

- They have to remember, if you are to achieve your end result, so:

  The 20-minute rule and keeping it digestible are particularly important;

  Use the breaks in your presenting to get them to practise what you have covered.

Questions: to clear any obstacles

- Take these as you go, because the audience is not going to learn if they have not understood.

- People learn better when training is interactive, but you may have to encourage them to participate actively.

- It is not only them asking you questions. You also ask questions, e.g. to get them thinking and to check what they have learned from you.

Conclusion: to check that they have learned

- Test out whether or not they have learned what you intended by getting them to do what you have taught them.

- This gives them an opportunity to practise, which will help them to remember.

In terms of the time breakdown this means that:

- *Body* and *questions* are combined and take about 70% of the time.

- *Introduction* (10%) and *conclusion* (20%) will normally require a little longer.

Again, these are rough guidelines.

Notes that help

In preparing your structure:

> Use key word notes, rather than a script, whenever possible.

If you have a script, it will tend to sound as though it is being read, unless you spend a lot of time rehearsing. You will find it easier to make your words come alive if you speak from notes. Another disadvantage of writing a script is that it is very time consuming.

You should be able to pick out the point you want, *at a glance*, then resume eye contact with your audience. Remember that you want to be able to find points easily when under pressure.

Here is an example:

Writing is *bold* and *easy to read*.

Each point is *visually separated* from the other points.

You can use the right hand column to incorporate 'stage directions' into your notes, written in a different colour. For example, when to use your visual aids, when to invite questions, timing.

You may find it helpful to write your notes on card(s) as they are easier to handle.

Strategy for success	
Why? – end result	
Presentation v training	
Who? – eyes of the audience	
The realistic test •　　**End result v ultimate aim**	
Positive **Logical** **You**	

4.0.3 Developing the structure

Before looking at how to develop the Structure for Success, we shall put it into context with the Strategy for Success. The two are shown diagramatically on the next page.

The diagram is in the form of three columns.

The sequence in which you *prepare a presentation* is identified by:

- Working *down* the first column, then the second and finally the third.

The thick line shows the sequence that you have to take the audience through to get them from:

- *How they see it now*, bottom of the first column, to

- *How they will have to see it*, top of first column.

Note that this path comes to an early end unless the Realistic Test is passed.

The first two columns, under the heading Strategy for Success, show the steps in preparing a successful presentation we have already considered in Section 3.

Note that you develop the content of the Structure for Success in the order:

- Conclusion

- Body

- Introduction.

This will probably seem to break the rule of being logical but the first thing to do is to be absolutely clear about how you will finish – your end result – if you are successful. This is your target, and the body of the presentation should lead up logically to this conclusion.

Why consider the introduction last? Remember that the purpose of the introduction is to *sell* to the audience the reasons for listening to your presentation. You cannot sell a product – your presentation – until you have designed it.

You use your introduction to lead the audience forward, making them want to hear what comes next, in this case the body. You must also ensure that there is a logical continuity for your audience. So, you must know the first point of information which you are to put across in the body **before** you can construct your introduction.

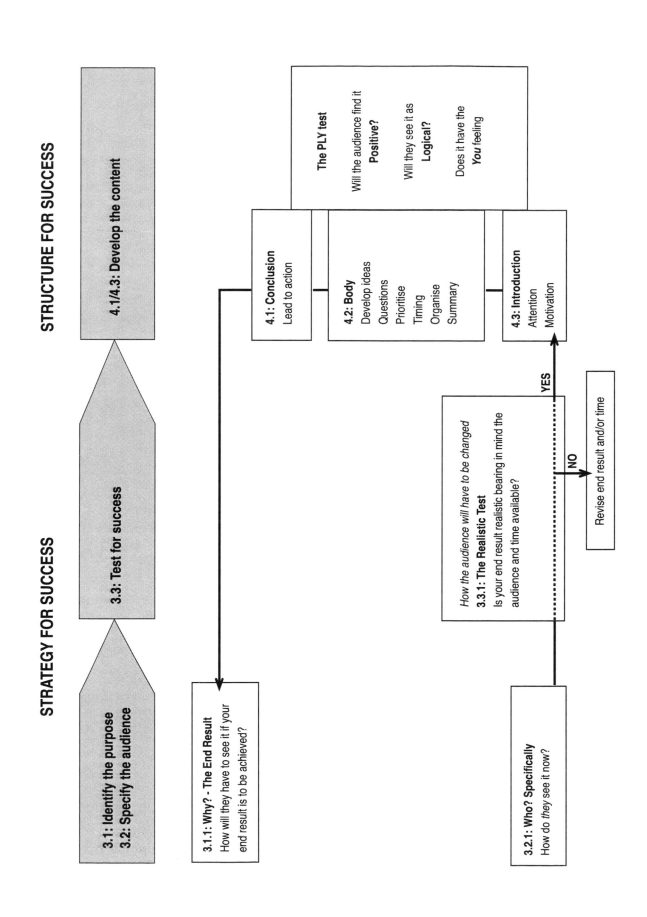

STRUCTURE FOR SUCCESS

4.1/4.3: Develop the content

STRATEGY FOR SUCCESS

3.3: Test for success

3.1: Identify the purpose
3.2: Specify the audience

3.1.1: Why? - The End Result
How will they have to see it if your
end result is to be achieved?

The PLY test

Will the audience find it **Positive?**

Will they see it as **Logical?**

Does it have the **You** feeling

4.1: Conclusion
Lead to action

4.2: Body
Develop ideas
Questions
Prioritise
Timing
Organise
Summary

4.3: Introduction
Attention
Motivation

How the audience will have to be changed
3.3.1: The Realistic Test
Is your end result realistic bearing in mind the
audience and time available?

YES

NO

Revise end result and/or time

3.2.1: Who? Specifically
How do *they* see it now?

4.1 Conclusion

Your *first* and *last* points are those that the audience will remember. So, make sure that you have a positive conclusion.

Persuasion

Use the conclusion to emphasise a positive end result and lead to action:

What do you want the audienoc to do next?

State the *outcome* you want from the presentation and the action required of the audience.

Make sure the action is as easy as possible for them to take.

Remember: the best time to get commitment is there and then.

Think of what you would say if the presentation has been successful.

Training

The conclusion is reached only when they have demonstrated that they can do what you wanted them to learn!

 Now go back to the presentation which you developed in the table on page 58. Decide on the action you are going to ask the audience to take and note it in the frame below.

The action I want the audience to take

Have you made the action as easy as possible for them to take?

4.2 Developing the body

No, this is not a printing error. You are not reading a workbook on fitness. This is where you have to decide **what** to say if you are to achieve your end result.

4.2.1 Produce your ideas

The answer to **what?** is not *'What shall I talk about?'* or *'What could I talk about?'* It is:

> **What** should you cover if you are to achieve your end result with your audience?

Answering this question means referring back to your:

- **Why**   see **3.1.1 Why? – The end result**, page 46
- **Who**   see **3.2.1 Who? – Specifically**, pages 51/52

If you are to achieve your end result, **what** do they need to know which they don't know already? In considering your answer:

- Think of any questions the audience might ask; give particular thought to questions you do not want! Try to think of 10 of these.

- Identify any areas where you might need to do further research, e.g. from books, magazines, or speaking to other people.

- Remember the key criteria:

  Positive focus

  Logical . . . to your audience;

  The *You* feeling

- Do not bother about the order in which you are going to say things you may want to change this once you have got the complete picture.

It is better to return to producing your ideas once or twice rather than trying to do it all at once. In this way, you often find a fresh approach which helps to generate new lines of thought.

If you are not sure about how to answer the question, use a brainstorming approach, ie:

- Take a blank sheet of paper and note any points which you might cover.

- Be open minded and let your ideas flow freely.

- Do not think in detail about the ideas, just note them down.

In fact, if you have time, it is always a good idea to use this brainstorming approach. It will help you to come up with ideas which you would not think of otherwise.

Mind mapping is another useful way to help you to produce your ideas; see Appendix C, page 113.

4.2.2 Prioritise your points

Now go through your points. Usually you will find that you have too much material for the time available so you will have to prioritise. You do this by referring back to the end result (see pages 46 and 55) and noting the points that your audience:

- *Must* be told: i.e. they are *essential* to achieving your end result.

The *'must be tolds'* are distinguished from those which:

- *Should* be told: points which are important to achieving your end result, but are not essential.

- *Could* be told: points which you would like to include, if there is time.

In deciding what you *must* and *should* cover, review those 10 questions you do not want. You may identify some which you are sure will be asked. It is usually better to answer these during the body of your presentation; you can then offset these 'weaker' points by both preceding and following them with the strengths of your case.

The next step is to estimate how long you think it will take to cover the *musts*:

> Most people underestimate how long it will take to cover their material.

4.2.3 Estimate the time

Point by point timing of your content gives you greater accuracy than trying to guess the length of the whole:

POINT BY POINT TIMING

Work out how long you think **each individual point** will take, then total those times.

Remember, if a point is important it is not sufficient just to state it. It will need to be given extra emphasis, for example: repeat it, put it another way, tell a story/give an example. You will have to allow for this when estimating your point by point timings.

Will you be able to cover all your *musts* within the time allocated?

• *YES:* then go on to add, in order of priority, your *shoulds* and finally your *coulds* until you have filled two-thirds of the total time allocated.	• *NO:* then there are two possible courses of action: Negotiate for more time, *or* Modify your *end result* to an end result which can be achieved within the time available.

> *Don't forget that the body is only two-thirds of the total time your presentation will take.*

Now go back to that imaginary presentation on the subject which you know well, page 58. In the frame on the next page go on to:

- Produce your ideas
- Select your priority points using point by point timing. Note the times in the right-hand column.

Remember the order does not matter at this stage.

Subject	_____
Audience	_____
Time	_____
Purpose	_____

Your points	Estimated time

4.2.4 Organise it

By this time you should have:

- Decided on *what* you are going to say, but not the order in which you are going to say it

- Checked that you can say it all within the time allocated.

The next task is to put it into order:

1. Decide how your material can be organised into sections which will help the audience to understand. Allocate headings for these sections.

2. Sort your material into the sections. Remember, people have a limited capacity to absorb information; *Seven points at a time is the absolute maximum*, i.e. the limit of what the audience can absorb at a time. However, to make points more memorable it is usually better to group them in *threes*, e.g. introduction, body and conclusion.

    However well you plan, you can never be *certain* of the actual time the presentation will take. For example, some groups ask more questions than others. It is advisable, therefore, to regard some of your *shoulds* as optional, i.e. you will cover them if you have time but could leave them out. Mark these very clearly in your notes.

3. Arrange the sections in an order which will be logical to your audience.

4. Check that this body:

    - Will achieve your end result (see pages 46 and 55);
      Satisfies the PLY test (see page 61).

    You may have done some of this organising as you were producing your ideas. In this case you should check out the finished product, particularly against the end result.

Note: Remembering the Attention Span, page 33:

You should plan to speak for no longer than 20 minutes without a break, e.g. for questions.

Now, organise the material you have decided to use for your imaginary presentation; note this in the frame on the next page.

Subject _____

Audience _____

Time _____

Purpose _____

Your *organised* points

•   Will the audience find this order logical?

You have now decided the:

- Body required to achieve your end result, and

- Order in which you are going to put it.

The next step is the summary.

4.2.5 Summary

Some people think of the summary as being part of the conclusion, indeed some close by merely summarising. We have identified the conclusion as having a more vital function: to lead to the action by triggering the end result and underlining the next step to be taken.

In fact there are usually *two different* points when it will help you to summarise:

1.   At the end of the body, to recap the key points you have made. This is necessary because some may not have been understood the first time, and some may have got lost in the minds of the audience. We refer to this as the summary.

2.   After questions as a lead-in to the conclusion, to remind the audience of any important points which you have dealt with during question time.

In a longer presentation, exceeding the 20-minute rule, you would add further summaries immediately before or after the breaks.

    For your imaginary presentation, identify the key points you want to remind your audience about and note them in the frame below.

Your summary

4.3 Attractive introduction

Yes, you really do produce this *after* your conclusion and body. If you are to be logical to your audience the introduction must flow smoothly into the body. It is only after you have produced the body that you know the first point you will be making in it. So it is only then that you know precisely where the introduction must lead to.

If you do not get their attention at the outset, you have lost the first trick; they've missed what you said and will need to catch up. But remember the attention span graph, page 33. It does not start at the top, you have to get them there! They have to tune in to listening to you.

How long this takes depends on you. That is why you should start to draw their attention to you before you start speaking. You then need to follow this with an attention grabbing message which gets the audience sitting up and taking notice of what you say. Your aim should be achieve this within the first minute.

4.3.1 Grab attention

The key to getting up to that attention span peak is to answer:

How will you grab the attention of your audience within 30 seconds?

What techniques might you use for grabbing attention? Make a list of those you can think of in the frame below.

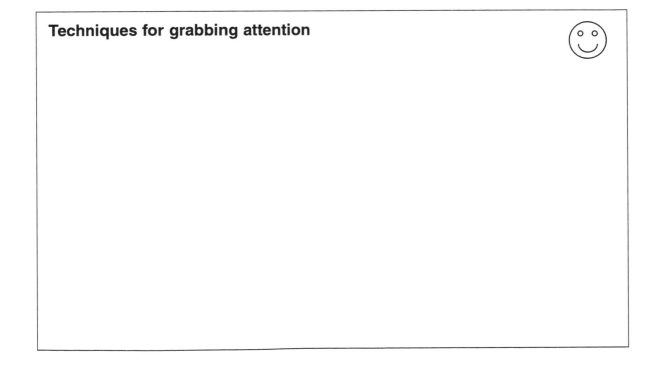

Some examples are:

- Make a surprising statement

- Arouse curiosity

- Tell an interesting story

- Ask a question

- Quote a famous person

- Use a strong visual/audiovisual aid

- Do something interesting or unusual.

You will probably create more of an impact by using two or three examples provided that they are consistent with each other.

You must get their attention, but will you keep it? That depends on whether or not you:

4.3.2 Get them motivated

The next key question is:

How will you motivate them to want to keep on listening?

You must prove to them that *your* presentation is going to be a worthwhile experience for *them*. You do this by:

- Establishing your credibility

- Showing you understand how they feel

- Highlighting what they will get out of listening to you

- Outlining points which you are sure will be of particular interest to them

- Highlighting any special items to expect.

4.3.3 Prepare them for what's to come

Note, you probably have not told them about your overall content yet. In this case your next step will usually, but not always, be to give them an outline of the structure of your presentation. They then have a 'map' which they can follow as you develop your points. It will help them to understand what you are talking about.

You may well have heard the old adage:

> "Tell them what you're going to tell them,
>
> tell them,
>
> then tell them what you've told them."

Generally this is good advice. However, it is not always a good idea. Telling them your objective, before they know why it is desirable, may stimulate them to resist what you are saying. This is most likely to be a factor when you are persuading; when you are training, the 'map' should help them to learn. So, think about whether it will help or hinder you to achieve your outcome. Include it at this point *unless* you think it will get in the way.

By this stage they will also want to know:

- How long you will take
- When you will be answering questions
- Whether or not there will be handouts.

These points must be covered because wondering about them could distract your audience if they do not know the answers. However, they do tend to disturb your continuity, so if someone else introduces you it may be better to get them to cover these points then.

 Return to the notes for the presentation which you developed in the frame on page 75. Focus particularly on the point which you decided that you would be making first. Note in the frame on the next page how you would:

- Grab the attention of your audience within 30 seconds
- Motivate them to *want* to listen to what you are going to say.

Ensure that this leads logically to that first point you are going to make.

Grab attention

Motivate

You started to plan a presentation on page 58 and have now completed the structure in the following stages:

Stage	Page	Content
Planned for success	58	Realistic purpose and audience
Produced the conclusion	69	Action you wanted the audience to take
Developed the body	75	Points to make, organised into headings and order
Summarised it	76	Repeat the key points
Created the introduction	80	Attention grabber and motivator for presentation

The PLY test

However hard you try, it is difficult to avoid looking at the content from your point of view when you get engrossed in working on it. So, before going any further you should apply the PLY test:

The PLY test

1.   Will *the audience* find your presentation **Positive**?

2.   Will *they* see it to be **Logical**?

3.   Does it have the **You** feeling?

Does the content of your presentation pass the PLY test?

If not, revise it so that it does.

The structure for Success

Keynotes

Develop your content in the following order:

CONCLUSION

To lead to action (4.0, p 63) check they have learned, (4.0, p 65)

If your end result is persuasion:

> State the action required of the audience, (**4.1**, p 69);

> Make sure it is as easy as possible for them to take, (**4.1**, p 69).

If your end result is training decide how to:

> Consolidate their learning, (**4.0**, p 65);

> Get them to demonstrate what they have learned, (**4.0**, p 65).

BODY

To prove the case (4.0, p 63) create learning, (4.0, p 65)

Answer: what should you cover if you are to achieve your end result with your audience? (**4.2.1**, p 70).

Brainstorm for ideas, (**4.2.1**, pp 70/71).

Prioritise by end result, (**4.2.2**, p 71).

Estimate the timing, (**4.2.3**, p 71).

Organise, from the audience's point of view, (**4.2.4**, p 74).

Produce your summary (**4.2.5**, p 76).

INTRODUCTION

To sell the presentation (4.0, p 63)/training, (4.0, p 64)

First, grab attention, (**4.3.1**, pp 77/78).

Then, motivate them to want to listen, (**4.3.2**, p 78).

5

From Content to Presentation

5.0 Introduction

5.1 Visual aids

5.2 Handling questions

5.3 Take control

5.4 And finally ...

5.0 Introduction

You are coach to a tennis star who is about to play a critical match. You've checked they have the right kit for the conditions, their supply of rackets (correctly strung), towels, bananas, etc. They are ready to go out and face their defeat. Are they really ready?

No, of course not! A coach knows that negative expectations are almost invariably fulfilled. So, they have to ensure that they send out their protégé expecting to win.

You are not properly prepared
until you can *visualise*

SUCCESS

This applies equally to you when you are going to give a presentation. So, just because you have prepared your content does not mean to say you are ready. There are several more things to do before you can visualise success.

5.0.1 Rehearse and refine

Rehearsing has two purposes it helps you to:

*   Check the material you have prepared

*   Build your confidence for the presentation.

So make the rehearsal a genuine test:

*   Stand up and speak it out loud.

You may feel stupid doing this, but only going through the presentation in your mind is not the same. Indeed it may be misleading, particularly with regard to timing.

As the word refine suggests, you may want to change it after this trial run. It is better to find this out before you spend time producing your visual aids.

Visual aids

People can be tempted to find out early in their planning what visual aids are available, commercially or otherwise. Avoid this! It can become difficult to resist the temptation to build the content around particularly good visual aids, rather than what is really needed to achieve the end result.

We consider visual aids, when and how to use them, more closely in Section 5.1.

Decide *precisely* how you will start

What will you do *just before* you start speaking?

You can improve your chance of grabbing attention by planning what you do before you start speaking. Standing there, waiting for people to stop talking means that different people give you their attention at different times; it is a stuttering start and can be embarrassing for the presenter. Make a definite change of scene, e.g. by standing up and moving toward the audience in a central position.

Rehearse with visual aids

You are not properly prepared to give your presentation until you have gone through it, using visual aids and notes as you intend to use them. So:

Rehearse,

Rehearse and

REHEARSE AGAIN!

You may find it useful to:

1.   Have a 'dummy run' in front of others.

2.   Record a 'dummy presentation' to hear how it sounds and, if video is available, to see how it looks.

As a result of rehearsing, you should be confident that your:

- Timing is right

- Visual aids work

- Notes give the right level of support.

You may find that you can use your visual aids as your notes, although this is *not* their primary function. Remember that it is better to have notes in easy to read, key word format, not as a script, see **Notes that help**, page 66.

If anyone else is involved in your presentation, e.g. in operating visual aids for you, have a rehearsal with them as well as on your own.

What about the questions?

Too many presentations fail even though well delivered and with the right content. The failure arises because the presenter 'lost it' at question time. We consider how to prepare for, and control questions in Section 5.2.

Take control . . . yourself

When you are presenting *you* are in the spotlight, whoever is nominally in charge. Do not leave someone else to set things up as they think it should be. Others may be able to give you useful advice, but *only you can decide what will work best for you*. So, decide how you want things to be set up and take steps to see that this is done. The more you can do to get things as you want them, the more you will get the feeling of being *at home*. This helps to make you feel more confident before you start.

The steps you can take are described in Section 5.3.

Some of the most common errors are: making the visual aid too complex, putting too much information on it, and using print which is too small to read. These are reminders of what not to do, but what about effective use?

 Think of examples of presenters using visual aids which have been particularly good in helping to get their message across through the sense of vision. Remember to include any examples which did not involve the usual visual aid equipment.

Effective use of visual aids

Thinking about other people's good ideas can help to trigger your own. This is important because, above all:

- Imagination is called for in producing effective visual aids.

Take the opportunity to look at advertisements and how graphics are used, for example in the television news, as further sources of ideas.

There are five basic principles to follow in the development of good visual aids:

- Do not let the visual aids take over
- Ensure they emphasise *key* points
- Use pictures to support your words
- Keep them clear and simple
- Make them add interest.

5.1.2 Don't let the visual aids take over

How often have you seen a presenter who showed a series of visual aids that were read to the audience! They might just as well have distributed copies for the audience to read in their own time, and at their own pace.

Even worse is the presenter who had the lights put out so that they could show a mass of 35mm slides! Possibly you cannot remember this because you soon dozed off, particularly if it was just after lunch! They would get better results using a few slides at a time, then inserting a blank so that they can draw the audience's attention back to them. They should also make sure they are actively pointing things out on the screen, thus bringing attention back to themselves.

It is up to the presenter to keep the attention of their audience, not let the visual aids take over. Visual aids should be tools which the presenter uses.

5.1.3 Ensure they emphasise *key* points

They should be used to assist your audience to understand and remember what your are presenting. So you should have:

> A visual aid for each of your *key* points.

In this way you help your audience to see the structure of your presentation.

Getting the emphasis right also means that you must decide *which part* of your visual aid you wish to highlight. Make this the focal point of attention and build the rest of the visual around it.

In the example below, the presenter, speaking at the end of 1996, is highlighting visually that the sales always go down in the first quarter of the year. So, although the overall trend is up, sales should be expected to drop in the first quarter of 1997.

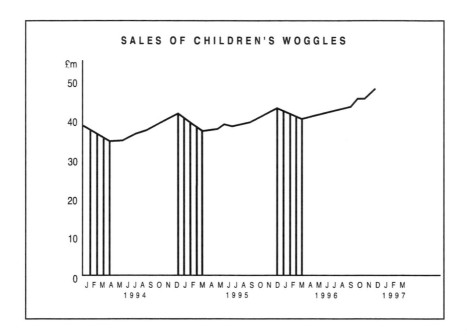

Emphasis can be created by making the best use of colour, white space, borders, contrasting backgrounds, etc.

When using a visual aid which contains only words and numbers, remember:

> It is difficult to have too few words and easy to have too many!

Think of ways to emphasise them, e.g.:

Italics / *Different print* / *point size*

Embolden

CAPITALS

Symbols

5.1.4 Use pictures to support your words

> *A picture speaks a thousand words.*

This may be a cliché but it is also the main reason why the visual sense has such power in absorbing information. A picture or graphic really does convey immediately what it would take many words to convey, incompletely.

The words *beautiful scenery* on the screen will do little to move an audience, but examples of that scenery may get them wanting to see it for themselves. The word *tranquillity* has little impact compared to a picture shot in diffused light. A slide with a bit of deliberate blur helps to reproduce the drama of sporting action.

The best visual aids are not just words: they express pictorially the message you are trying to get across. The best thing is to have a picture or chart which represents the point you are making verbally (see page 90 for an example). If you do have to fall back on words, think how to introduce a pictorial element, e.g. through the use of colour, boxes and bullets.

5.1.5 Keep them clear and simple

Visual aids are to help your audience understand, so you must ensure that they are:

*   Uncluttered and easy to read.

Of course, easy to read means that they must be legible. It is a pity that not all presenters remember this.

It also means limiting the amount of information on them. For example, do not try to show a table of figures: instead, select the most important features and show them diagramatically. In addition, this will give you a 'picture' to support your words.

A visual aid with words only should have a:

*   Heading and no more than eight lines on it if in portrait
*   Heading and no more than six lines on it if in landscape.

5.1.6 Use them to add interest

Visual aids should add interest and variety to your presentation. All too often this aspect is undermined by the presenter using a monotonous repetition of visuals in the:

> same colour using the same print in the
>
> same size with the
>
> same spacing

Colour associations can also be used to help express your message:

Red   danger; aggression; excitement

Yellow   sun; gold; summer

Green   safety; freshness; outdoors

Blue   tranquillity; water/sea/sky; authority.

The perception of colour depends on its proximity to other colours, so a warm colour (red or amber) appears closer when next to a cooler colour (blue or green). This is why blue is so often chosen as a background colour for visual aids.

Adding interest, rather than distracting, also means that the visual should look right. Ensure that the layout of your visual aids is balanced and in harmony.

You may need to consider whether landscape or portrait is most appropriate to achieve this. However, if you do mix the two, remember to take this into account when you set things up for the presentation.

5.1.7 Synchronisation

It is one thing to produce visual aids which follow the principles, but this, in itself, does not make them effective. They are some of the presenter's tools and, like all tools, must be used properly. It is essential to see that:

> Each visual aid is synchronised with what the presenter is saying.

Achieving this means that you should:

Withhold	the visual aid until you are ready to talk about it
Show	it to support and give emphasis to what you are saying
Remove	it as soon as you have finished talking about it, to avoid it becoming a distraction.

This means you have to consider:

- When it should be shown – *precisely*

- If it should be shown complete, or in parts at a time, the principle also applies to any part of a visual aid

- How long your audience will need to absorb what is shown. This may mean quite a long pause if, for example, you are showing something they will have to read.

5.1.8 Selection of media

In these days of rapidly advancing technology, it is almost impossible to provide details of all the equipment available. It is also in danger of becoming out of date almost as soon as it is printed!

The important thing for you to do is to find out what you have available, both in terms of equipment and computer programmes for the production of visual aids. However, be selective in how you use software packaged solutions; remember, the most effective visual aids call for imagination.

You may have access to some or all of the following basic types of visual aid equipment, together with differing levels of sophistication in how they can be used:

Board (white)	Primarily for recording during the presentation, may also have stick-on (magnetic) facility.
Flipchart	Also primarily for recording during the presentation or when nothing else can be used. It is small scale in comparison to the board but a visual can be removed from view without losing it.
Overhead projector	A flexible, readily available piece of equipment. Can be rather cumbersome to use; more sophisticated variations using computer based material are often used instead.
Slide projector	Has a more refined optics system than the overhead projector which means it is better for photographs and for larger audiences.

| *Film/Video* | For audiovisuals with movement. This does take over from the presenter while it is being shown, so make sure you introduce it and lead out of it when you resume. |

In deciding which equipment to use for a particular presentation you need to consider:

- How you want to use visual aids to help get your message across. For example, pre-prepared or produce on the spot, photographic (still or moving).

- How important it is to project a quality image

- The status of your audience

- Their expectations

- The budget available for production costs

- How often the visual aid is likely to be used

- The facilities which are available for the presentation and those which *could* be.

Another important factor to consider is:

- How many different media should you use?

It is advisable to have a limit of two different pieces of visual aid equipment. Using more can be distracting for you as well as for the audience, as it causes concern about which to use next.

If you have visual aids which involve using more than two media it may be better to:

- Transfer some of the aids to another medium so that you can consolidate what you use

- Have a break in your presentation so that you can switch the equipment.

5.1.9 Golden rules for any visual aid used

- **Rehearse**

Never show a visual aid without first testing it and integrating it into your presentation. This is essential, to check out:

- That is does the job you want.

- The timing: when to show it, when to remove it

- Additions you may need, e.g. blank slides.

- The overall time you will take, allowing for the visual aids.

It helps your confidence if you are using something you have tried and tested already.

If someone else is going to operate the visual aids for you, have a run through with them.

- **Contingency**

Have a back-up plan in case the equipment does not work.

- **Check the equipment**

Make sure that you are familiar with the controls on the particular equipment that you are using – they vary from one model to another.

- **Check the layout**

Do make certain that all the audience will be able to see all the visual aids. It is very easy to overlook the fact that you may be standing in the way, or that an OHP head may be obscuring their view.

The last thing you did with the presentation you have been preparing was to produce the introduction, see page 80.

Your next tasks are to decide:

- Where you want to include a visual aid

- What medium you would use

- Design each visual aid.

Visual aids

Keynotes

- Make sure you are using visual aids, not visual distractions, (**5.1.1**, pp 86/87).

- The sense of vision is the 75% sense for absorbing information, (**5.1.1**, p 86).

The principles of effective visual aids

- Don't let the visual aids take over, (**5.1.2**, p 89).

- Ensure they emphasise *key* points, (**5.1.3**, pp 89/90).

- Use pictures to support your words, (**5.1.4**, p 91).

- Keep them clear and simple, (**5.1.5**, p 91).

- They should *add* interest, (**5.1.6**, p 92).

Each visual aid must be synchronised with what the presenter is saying, (**5.1.7**, pp 92/93).

Know about media available to you and select for the job, (**5.1.8**, pp 93/94).

Remember the golden rules, (**5.1.9**, p 95):

- Rehearse

- Contingency

- Check the equipment

- Check the layout.

5.2 Handling questions

 The success of a presentation can be undermined completely by the failure of the presenter to handle questions effectively. Think about your own experience as a member of the audience. What have you seen a presenter say or do about questions which has been counterproductive to their presentation? In the frame below note the things they did and the effect they had.

Ineffective handling of questions	
What they did	*Its effect on the audience*

The following table covers some of the most frequently mentioned problems:

What they did	Its effect on the audience
Did not let the audience know when they could ask questions.	Distracted by thinking about what to do.
Discouraged questions.	Dissatisfied.
Answered the person who shouted loudest.	Gave up trying to put question, unless you were the loudest!
Did not give you the chance to ask the question you wanted to.	Dissatisfied, as a result may be uncommitted to the presenter's desired end result.
Used planted questions (see page 99).	Suspicious, what else have they got to hide?
Waffled around the question without answering it.	Lost credibility, did not seem to know the subject.
Answered a different question.	Dissatisfied.
Gave a long, rambling answer.	Switched off.
Got involved with one person in the audience.	Felt excluded and then frustrated.
Argued with the questioner.	Presenter lost credibility.
Overran.	Started thinking about what they should be doing next.

You may have other points as well. It underlines how important it is to answer questions effectively if you want to achieve your end result. You will not achieve this without careful preparation, including deciding when to take questions.

There are principles to remember for handling questions effectively:

- Be seen to *welcome* them

- Keep *control*, it is easier than having to regain it

- Keep *everyone* involved

- Keep the audience on our side

- Keep the answers to the point

- Finish on time.

5.2.1 Prepare for questions

Awkward questions

We have already identified that to think through the kind of questions you may get is an essential part of preparing and developing your ideas about the body of your presentation, Section 4.2.1, page 70.

- Give particular thought to questions you do not want! **Think of 10 of them.**

We also highlighted that if you are sure you are going to have to deal with the point it is usually better to *anticipate* the question. Answer it during your presentation, Section 4.2.2, page 71.

This will still leave several which you have not yet covered. You may not get them but supposing you do? It is much easier to think of good answers to difficult questions in advance than get caught out when in front of the audience.

> Decide how you would answer that question, then
> rehearse your answer.

Awkward questioners

Do you know of anyone in the audience who may be difficult?

> Decide how you would deal with them,
> then rehearse your solution.

No questions

Suppose there are no questions, what will you do? You know that often the problem is getting the first one; when that hurdle is overcome they start flowing. Here it is useful to think of one or two questions which you would like, some of those *'shoulds'* which you decided you did not have time to include.

You can then use them to stop that uncomfortable silence building up by introducing them as the first question: "just while you are thinking of your questions, one of the points I am often asked about is . . ."

Planted questions are seldom a good idea. It requires a lot of practice with the plant if you are to make sure that it is not obvious; remember those used planted questions which had the effect of making people suspicious: 'what else have they got to hide?' Plants have also been known to forget they are meant to be asking a question or to ask the wrong one.

5.2.2 When should you take questions?

Another point in your preparation is to decide when you are going to take questions. You may do this as you go or at fixed points of your own choosing. There is no 'right answer' as to which procedure to adopt. There are advantages and disadvantages to each:

Advantages of taking questions as you go along

- Enables your audience to check immediately if there is a point which they do not understand

- Your audience does not have the potential distraction of thinking about their question until 'Question Time'

- Avoids your audience forgetting a question

- Creates better involvement

- Provides better feedback for the presenter.

Advantages of fixed periods for questions

- Retains the sequence of your points

- May be easier for your audience, as a whole, to follow

- Easier to control

- Avoids potential disruption to your timing.

Decide when you will take questions by considering the relative importance of these points. As a guide, it is usually better to:

- Take questions *as you go along* if you are a trainer.

- Have *fixed* question periods if you are trying to *persuade* your audience.

However, there are times when other factors may 'decide' for you – the size of your audience, for instance.

Having made the decision, you must make sure right at the beginning that the audience is told, by yourself or the chairperson, that you will be taking questions and when.

5.2.3 Be seen to *welcome* them

Most people feel apprehensive and unsure when the time comes to answer questions and they are glad when it is over. You can rehearse your presentation to the point where you feel sure that you know what's going to happen. With questions, however, you can never be certain. There's always the chance that somebody is going to ask one you have not thought about. Will you be able to cope?

But think how you would feel if you do not get any questions. There is an uncomfortable silence does it mean that:

- They didn't understand
- They were bored
- It was pitched too low
- It was pitched too high
- They disagree
- They agree and really don't have anything to ask?

You are doubtful and uncertain: what do you do next?

Some audiences may be reluctant to ask questions: perhaps because they are concerned about showing their ignorance, or find it difficult to stop the presenter who is in full flow. You may have to work at encouraging them before you get a response.

Remember, you set out to get your audience to do something as a result of your presentation. When you have presented the body, some may still be undecided. You have to find out about this before you can do anything about it. Questions help **you** to identify their doubts and resolve them by:

- Dealing with any problems they see
- Clearing up any misunderstanding.

They can also indicate any further action that may be necessary on your part by:

- Showing how well your content has been received.

So, although a bit of you feels that you do not want questions, it is in your own interests to:

> Welcome questions
>
> and
>
> be seen to do so.

5.2.4 *Keep control*, it's easier than having to regain it

For some, questions are a relief. They feel more comfortable when interacting with their audience and they no longer feel that they are in the spotlight. They often start to behave more like themselves and look more relaxed. It is important to remember that:

- Control passes to the questioner whilst they put their question.

At this point it is *they* who are directing what is going to be said next. So the presenter must ensure that they are in control both immediately before and immediately after the question.

Immediately before

Be careful about letting the audience call out a question whenever they feel they want to. It can easily degenerate into both you and the audience losing the structure of the points you are making. The audience may also see it as answering the person who shouted loudest!

Immediately after

Pay particular attention to making sure you:

> Take control back once the question has been put.

If the presenter relaxes and does come out of the spotlight, they can suddenly find that the questioner has retained the control which they *should* have had only momentarily.

Use the sequence shown on the next page to help you to retain control:

Control sequence

• Face the questioner and **listen**	Let them finish! Interrupt only if the question becomes lengthy and rambling or is not relevant to the presentation. When this happens ask questions to refocus your questioner. Satisfy yourself that you understand the question.
• **Pause** . . . for the length of time it takes to say slowly: 1000, 2000, 3000, i.e. approximately three seconds	This is very important because it: • Creates a break during which you *regain control from the questioner* • Gives you thinking time before your answer. You cannot unsay your first sentence once you have said it!

• Ensure that the whole of your audience has:
    Heard the question;
    Understood it.
	If you have any doubt about either of these points, rephrase and repeat the question; check with the questioner that you have got it right.

• Answer the question, fully but concisely.	Do not ramble. Unless the answer is very brief, speak to all your audience. This: • Gets the focus of attention back to you. • Helps you to keep everyone's attention.
• Check with the questioner.	For example, 'Does that answer your question?'

You need to *know* how long three seconds is without thinking about it. You can then *use* the time to think about your answer. Get this time ingrained in your mind by:

Practising saying 1000, 2000, 3000 slowly, timing it as you do so.

5.2.5 Keep *everyone* involved

We are conditioned to speak to the person who has put a question to us, because it is what we do in normal conversation. It is very natural, therefore, to follow this practice when answering a question from a member of the audience.

Natural, but dangerous: in a presentation you are both leaving them in control and losing contact with the rest of the audience. While you are looking at just one person you lose sight of what is happening to the others: are they following, getting bored or irritated? You must retain eye contact all round so that you can respond quickly to the early warning signals.

5.2.6 Keep the audience on your side

This relates to keeping everyone involved and knowing how they are reacting. If you are alert to their messages you know when they are getting fed up with an awkward or persistent questioner.

You can enlist their help to deal with the situation, e.g. by asking if anyone else has any questions. If you have judged it right they will respond eagerly and you will be able to say: "As there are several other people with questions I suggest we discuss this further over coffee."

If you want to keep them on your side do not argue; state your own point firmly and politely. If this does not work, agree to differ. Always be the person who is being reasonable and never lose your temper.

5.2.7 Keep it to the point

This applies both to what you say in answering and to the questions themselves.

Your answers

Remember, in the audience's perception you might be seen as waffling around without answering, addressing different questions and giving a long rambling reply. Also, if you spend too long on some people's questions you may end up stopping others from asking theirs; try to be fair, as well as to the point.

It is easier for people to ask you for more information than for them to stop you saying too much. So it is better for you to err on the side of brevity rather than going on too long.

Their questions

You may be asked something which is not relevant. You might think it is easy enough to answer, but beware of doing so. It can lead to a series of questions which move the presentation further and further away from the point. It is better to remind the audience of the reason for your presentation, show politely that the question is not relevant to this and offer to discuss it after you have finished.

5.2.8 Finish on time

Remember that it is your responsibility to finish on time. If you do not you will lose your audience in thought, if not in their physical presence. Once they start thinking you are going to overrun, their minds will turn to what they should be doing next.

You may be running out of time when it is apparent that there are more questions. You have two alternatives:

- To close, but at the same time show that you are aware that there are other questions and tell people how they can put them to you, e.g. after the presentation;

- To seek agreement to extend the presentation, but be sure that this is *willingly* given.

5.2.9 And questions about questions

What if you do not know the answer? Some people advocate that you should bluff it out. This is very dangerous. You may be very good at it and get away with it as often as 19 times out of 20; you *are* very good at it if you are as successful as this! But what about that twentieth time when you didn't get away with it? Your credibility is damaged and the news gets round.

So when you do not know the answer it is better to say so . . *and*

- Promise that you will find out and let the questioner know

   or, if this is not practical

- Tell the questioner where to find the answer.

 Now let us go back to that presentation you have been tackling as you went through this workbook and consider what you need to do to prepare for questions:

- Have you thought of 10 questions you do not want?

- Have you answered the ones you are sure you will get, during the body?

- Decide how you would answer the others; rehearse answering the most difficult ones, using the process described in Section 5.2.4, p 102.

- Decide what you would do if there were no questions.

- Decide when you would take questions.

5.2.10 Questions – in conclusion

 What about those tips that you can gain from observing others' successes? What have you seen a presenter say or do about questions which worked well? In the frame below, note the things they did and the effect that they had.

Successful handling of questions ☺	
What they did	*Its effect on the audience*

Handling questions

Keynotes

- Prepare by planning for awkward questions, awkward questioners, and no questions, (**5.2.1**, p 99).

- Decide when you are going to take questions and let the audience know, (**5.2.2**, p 100).

The principles for handling questions

- Be seen to *welcome* them, (**5.2.3**, p 101).

- *Keep control*, it is easier than having to regain it, (**5.2.4**, p 102).

- When answering use the handling questions sequence, (**5.2.4**, p 102) – Listen; Pause – 1000, 2000, 3000; ensure everyone understands the question; answer fully but concisely, to everyone; check the question has been answered.

- Keep *everyone* involved, (**5.2.5**, p 104).

- Keep them on your side, (**5.2.6**, p 104).

- Keep it to the point, (**5.2.7**, p 104).

- Finish on time, (**5.2.8**, p 105).

If you do not know the answer, say so but offer to find out, (**5.2.9**, p 105).

5.3 Take control

Always work on the principle that:

> When you are presenting you are in charge
>
> and
>
> Arrange things as you want them.

You have got to do this if you are to achieve your best results. You will also find that the more you can do to get things as you want, then the more at home you feel. Of course, there may be limits as to how far you can go: there may be objections to knocking down that wall, dismantling the stage or you may be one of a number of presenters and have to fit in with the requirements of the others.

The principle 'take control' still applies, even if it does have to be within limits. Sometimes it may mean no more than spending a couple of minutes getting things set up when you are following another speaker. In this case, warn the audience so that they can occupy themselves with something other than making you feel uncomfortable because they are watching your every move.

If you are to take control there is further preparation involved. It is worthwhile to produce check lists so that you do not have to try and remember everything at a time when you will be trying to concentrate on other things. The Appendices will help you to produce the check lists, which should cover:

- What needs to be done *In advance* of the presentation, Appendix A, p 111.

- What needs to be done *On the day* of the presentation, Appendix B, p 112.

- What needs to be done *immediately before you start*, Appendix B, p112.

5.4 And finally . . .

You have spent some time going through this workbook and on developing the presentation which you started on page 58. Following this process should help when you next have to prepare a presentation.

But why not carry the work you have put in to fruition? What about the final exercise?

- Arrange a time and place for a group of people who match your imaginary audience, see page 58.

- Aim to do this as soon as possible while the work you have done is fresh in your mind. Set a date *now.*

- Rehearse, see pages 83/84.

- Prepare and use your checklists, see (Appendices A, page 111 and B, page 112).

- Give the presentation to them.

- Ask them for feedback on how it came across to them, see page 32.

Learning about presentations never ends!

Further study

There are some suggestions for further reading in Appendix C, page 113. One avenue you may find particularly useful is NLP which can help you in your presenting and in:

Learning from others' experience.

Watch out for what you can learn from seeing others giving presentations. Note:

- What goes wrong, or does not seem to work and think about how you can ensure that it will not happen to you

- What does work well for them. Try to get an opportunity to speak to them about it, so that you get a better idea about how to make it work for you.

Learning from your experience

The most important learning of all, so grab all the opportunities you can. To make sure it really is learning from experience:

- In future when you give a presentation, find the time to think about how it went as soon as possible afterwards. Note what:

  - Went well, so you can use it again

  - You were not so happy with, and think about how you could do it differently next time.

Add any new points in the relevant frames as you notice them: they are indexed in your personal record at the front of the workbook.

> **Good luck with your presentations,**
>
> **may all your audiences do**
>
> **what you want them to as a result!**

Appendices

A In advance checklist
B On the day checklist
C For further reading

Appendix A

In advance checklist

> Remember Murphy's Law: If something can go wrong, it will.

If you do not know the venue, you should, whenever possible, go and see it as part of your preparation. Also, when possible, have a rehearsal at the venue. This will enable you to anticipate any problems which may arise and give you the confidence of having done it there.

Layout
How big is it?

What is the set-up, for example: lectern, platform? Is this what you want?

What is the seating arrangement? Does this encourage 'us v them', formality or informality?

For the audience
Is it adequately ventilated?

How comfortable is the seating (uncomfortable or too comfortable!)?

Distractions
What potential distractions are there (through window, noises outside the room, etc.

Microphone
Will you need one? If so, check how it should be matched to your voice, *before* the presentation.

Lighting
Will this have a soporific effect?

Will it impair the impact of any of your visual aids?

Is it likely to be affected by weather, e.g. bright sunlight on the screen?

How can it be controlled?

Visual aids
How will you use them so everyone can see?

Will they do the job you want?

Are you familiar with the controls on the equipment?

What will you do if they fail?

Electric points
Where are they?

Are there enough?

Will you need extension leads?

What needs to be done to ensure that the leads are not a safety hazard?

What type of plug will be required?

Appendix B
On the day checklist

Arrive early!

If you could not see the venue in advance, arrive even earlier so that you can go through the *In advance* checklist.

Advance checks   Did you have any special arrangements to be made, e.g. to avoid outside distractions? Check that they have been done.

Layout   Is this as you decided it should be?

Are you sure that everyone will be able to see your visual aids?

Electric points   Are all the ones you need working?

Lighting   Are all the lights working?

Visual aids   Check the equipment:

Is it all working *completely* i.e. including back-up such as second bulb on OHP?

Is it as easy as possible for you when using it, e.g. good size surface for your transparencies close to the OHP?

Have you got the right pens, etc. available? Do they work?

You   Have you got some water available?

Have you worked out how you are going to start, e.g. from where will you speak?

Have you got rid of any potential distractions, e.g. coins in pocket, clinking earrings?

Now finalise your *Immediately before you start* checklist:

Visual aid equipment correctly aligned and focused, water, check time, etc.

These are some items only.
The list will depend on your earlier checks and the needs for the particular presentation.

Appendix C
For further reading

Communication and speaking

Communicate with confidence Dianna Booher, 1994, McGraw-Hill Inc, New York, ISBN 0 07 006606 X

How to Speak Without Fear Natalie Rogers, 1984, Ward Lock Limited, London, ISBN 0 7063 6301 9

Secrets of Successful Speakers Lilly Walters, 1993, McGraw-Hill Inc, New York, ISBN 0 07 068034 5

Body language

Bodily Communication Michael Argyle, 1988, Methuen, London and New York, ISBN 0 416 38150 2

Body Language: How to Read Other's Thoughts by Their Gestures Allan Pease, 1984, Sheldon Press, London, ISBN 0 85969 406 2.

Your image and your voice

Your Total Image Philippa Davies, 1990, Piatkus, London, ISBN 0 86188 842 1

The Right to Speak – Working with the Voice Patsy Rodenburg, 1992, Methuen Drama, London, ISBN 413 66130 x

The Image Factor Eleri Sampson, 1996, Kogan Page, London, ISBN 0 7494 2101

Mindmap

The Mind Map Book Tony Buzan with Barry Buzan, 1996, BBC Books, London. ISBN 0 563 37101 3

Neuro Linguistic Programming – NLP

Frogs into Princes Richard Bandler and John Grindler, 1990, Eden Grove Editions, Enfield, Middlesex, ISBN 1 870845 03 X

NLP at Work Sue Knight, 1995, Nicholas Brealey Publishing, London, ISBN 1 85788 070 6